RELIGION IN CONTEMPORARY DEBATE

BOOKS BY ALAN RICHARDSON
Published by The Westminster Press

Religion in Contemporary Debate
History, Sacred and Profane
The Bible in the Age of Science
A Preface to Bible Study

Religion
in Contemporary Debate

by
ALAN RICHARDSON

THE WESTMINSTER PRESS
Philadelphia

LIBRARY OF CONGRESS CATALOG CARD No. 66-22987

Published by The Westminster Press ®
Philadelphia, Pennsylvania

PRINTED IN THE UNITED STATES OF AMERICA

CONTENTS

Foreword   9

1 Is Religion a Good Thing?   13
   The rationalist criticism of religion   13
   Religion and the human sciences   15
   The theological onslaught upon religion   17
   'Religionless' Christianity   19
   The biblical attack upon religion   21
   The Christianizing of religion   26

2 Religion as the Abolition of the Secular   30
   The Christian definition of religion   30
   The non-Christian religions   33
   Secular Christianity   36
   Secularism   40
   Secularization   42
   The Christian presupposition of secularization   45

3 Varieties of Religious Atheism   49
   Speculative religiosity   49
   Existentialism in an atheistic mode   52
   Empiricism in a religious mode   56
   The Christian significance of atheism   60

4 Cosmology and Language   65
   The biblical world-view and modern scientific
      cosmology   66
   How far should we demythologize?   69
   That which cannot be demythologized   74
   Words and the Word   77

5 The New Hermeneutics   81
    The earlier Heidegger   81
    The later Heidegger   85
    The hermeneutic problem   89
    The new hermeneutic   91
    When words are events   94

6 The Death of God: A Report Exaggerated   102
    Can we prove the existence of God?   103
    Why doesn't God demonstrate his existence?   106
    Hearing and hearsay   108
    Grace and anti-grace   113
    Beyond humanism   117

Index of Names   123

FOREWORD

THE six chapters of this book contain lectures given in Queen's College Hall, Dundee, between November 17 and 24, 1965. They are substantially in the form in which they were delivered, with a slight expansion in two or three places. They constitute the first of what is intended to be an annual series of lectures on religion, this term being used in the broadest sense, including religions other than Christianity and being open to treatment from every point of view. It seemed to me appropriate that the first lecture of the series should be devoted to a discussion of the meaning of the word 'religion' itself, and that the following lectures should deal with some of the main issues raised in the debate which is being so vigorously carried on today, more particularly about the Christian religion. The honour done to me by the Master and the Council of Queen's College in inviting me to be the first lecturer in the series is acknowledged by the dedication of this book, which also is intended to express the sincere gratitude of my wife and myself to the Principal of St Andrew's University, Sir Malcolm Knox; the Master of Queen's College, Professor A. A. Matheson, Q.C.; the Queen's College Council; the members of the Committee for Lectures on Religion; the Chaplain to Queen's College, the Rev. Graeme M. Bruce, and to many other kind friends who helped to make our sojourn in Dundee so happy and memorable.

St Andrew's Day, 1965   ALAN RICHARDSON

RELIGION IN CONTEMPORARY DEBATE

1

IS RELIGION A GOOD THING?

'RELIGION' is one of the slipperiest words in the dictionary. It covers so many different things and has so many different emotional overtones. Whether you think religion a good thing or a bad thing will depend upon what kind of religion you have encountered and what you consider its essence to be. Many of the wisest and most God-fearing men of past ages, and some of the leading theologians of our own day, unhesitatingly declare that religion is a bad thing.

The Rationalist Criticism of Religion

Ever since the dawn of rational thinking in Ionia philosophers have maintained a critical attitude towards religion. Xenophanes (c. 576-484 BC) attacked unworthy notions and legends of the gods; Homer and Hesiod, he said, ascribed all kinds of disgraceful conduct to the gods, including thefts and adulteries. He pointed out that men create the gods in their own image: Africans make their gods black and snub-nosed; the Thracians say theirs have blue eyes and red hair. If horses and lions could paint, their gods would look like horses and lions. From the very beginnings of European thought, we might say, a beneficent dispensation of providence has decreed that there should always be rationalistic thinkers at hand to ridicule the crudities of popular religion. Plato himself, who counselled reverence towards the gods and wished to improve their public image, wanted Homer

13

and Hesiod banned from the school curriculum and echoed the verdict of the philosophers who said that the poets should be horsewhipped.

It was Greek philosophy rather than Greek religion which generated concern for moral issues. In much popular religion the gods were everyday familiars, rather like television personalities today; everyone talked about their latest manifestations, and, after all, their private goings-on were their own affair and were not necessarily to be imitated by ordinary mortals. The gods were not interested in ethical conduct, though they were jealous of their own prestige; a prudent man would pay them proper respect. Fear of the gods and their revenges constituted a large element in Greek religion; the fear of hell was as strong in pagan Greece as it was in Victorian England. Epicurus (341-270 BC), in the former period, and Bertrand Russell, who was brought up in the latter, sought to allay this fear with the aid of contemporary physical science. Armed with the atomic theory of Democritus, Epicurus reasoned that death meant the disintegration of our bodily structure, and hence there was no need to dread an after-life in which the gods could torment us for our neglect of them. Bertrand Russell, relying upon a similar argument from physics, urged that the recognition that death means total annihilation robs it of its terror: there is nothing to be afraid of in going to sleep.[1] The fear of the supernatural, which gave occasion to all the crudities and cruelties of religion, could thus be abolished for ever. Lucretius (99-55 BC), the Roman poet who turned the rather dull philosophy of Epicurus into vivid and imaginative poetry, spoke for a long succession of rationalistic philosophers in his well-known line, *Tantum religio potuit suadere malorum:* so much that is evil was religion able to induce.[2]

---

[1] *What I Believe*, London, 1925.
[2] *De Rerum Natura*, i. 101.

Is Religion a Good Thing?

Religion and the Human Sciences

This short and easy way by which rationalism proposes to abolish the fear of the supernatural does not, however, succeed in abolishing religion as such. We can perhaps see why this is so if we pause to ask what gives rise to this universal human phenomenon of religion. Though it has sometimes been maintained that certain primitive peoples, such as the Andaman islanders, were entirely without any form of religion, the growth of ethnological knowledge tends to show that in fact religion is a phenomenon common to all peoples at every stage of cultural development. Before we attempt a definition of religion, it would therefore seem sensible to ask what gives rise to this distinctively human phenomenon. There appears to be a large measure of agreement amongst theologians, anthropologists and philosophers in answering this question. Briefly we might say that two principal factors are involved. First, there is the virtually universal recognition of a need for salvation from the condition into which human beings are born—thrown, as Heidegger would say, into the universe and there 'abandoned for death'. Secondly, there is the universal recognition that we are all running out of time. In adolescence most of us are less conscious of this, but with every year of adult life we become increasingly aware in an acutely personal way of the insecurity of our existence and the inevitability of senescence, decay and death. The Psalmist voiced a universal human concern: 'Lord, let me know mine end, and the number of my days, that I may be certified how long I have to live. . . . For man walketh in a vain shadow . . . he heapeth up riches and cannot tell who shall gather them' (Ps. 39.5-7). Bertrand Russell's gospel of physical science does nothing to assuage this deeply human anxiety. In an essay written in 1903 he pronounced the doom of every human aspiration, affirming it to be 'nearly certain' that 'all the labours of the

15

ages, all the devotion, all the inspiration, all the noonday brightness of human genius, are destined to extinction in the vast death of the solar system, and that the whole temple of Man's achievement must inevitably be buried beneath the débris of a universe in ruins'.[1]

We may, then, offer one kind of definition of religion, but we must remember that definitions are never totally adequate. A definition is adequate only from the point of view of a particular purpose: a musician and a physicist would define a chord in different ways, and each would be right from the point of view of his own interest. From an anthropological or sociological standpoint it would be adequate to define religion as man's response to the exigency of the human condition, in which he is driven to seek security, status and permanence by identifying himself with a reality greater, more worthy and more durable than himself. Some such definition is more adequate than one which defines religion in terms of man's relation to the supernatural, because the existence of the supernatural is not a matter of which the human sciences as such can take cognizance. Moreover, besides covering the great ethnic religions, such as Buddhism, Shintoism or Islam, it covers also primitive animistic religion, nature religion, the ancient mystery religions, and also such modern 'religions' of the industrial era as fascism and communism. Religion, from this point of view, represents man's endeavour to come to terms with the realities of his condition with the object not only of making them more bearable but also of assuring himself that there is significance in his existence. The human sciences are not concerned with assessing the validity or truth-value of particular religious systems, but it is arguable that in so far as a religion is successful in helping its adherents to adjust their life to reality, its ideas may be

[1] The essay, entitled 'The Free Man's Worship', was reprinted in *Philosophical Essays*, London, 1910, 59ff.

deemed to possess a measure of truth.[1] But there is always the possibility of developing the counter-argument that religion is at best only an escape-fantasy invented to compensate men for the misery of their lot and at worst a hindrance to their efforts to improve it. All such arguments are two-edged; Marxism, which has developed the latter theory, has succeeded only in replacing the myth of heaven with the Utopian myth of the classless society after the revolution. Questions about the truth or falsity of religion are beyond the scope of the social and anthropological sciences, including the comparative study of religion; all that these disciplines can do is to describe and compare the various religious responses of different human cultures to the fundamental anxiety which at every stage of human development has given rise to those attitudes which are classed as religious.

The Theological Onslaught upon Religion

It is the character of religion as a human response to the wretchedness of the human condition which has led in recent times to the sharp attack upon religion made by certain theologians. The most famous contemporary theological teacher, Karl Barth, has allied himself with the rationalist philosophers and the Marxists in dismissing religion as a bad thing. In his massive *Kirchliche Dogmatik* he has a very long section headed 'The Revelation of God as the Abolition of Religion'.[2] He distinguishes between the Christian faith, which is based solely upon God's revelation of himself in Jesus Christ, and all religion, which is man's futile search for ultimate truth and meaning. This search is doomed to failure, because God is the Wholly Other, and if

[1] On this question see W. Montgomery Watt, *Truth in Religion*, Edinburgh, 1963.
[2] Eng. trans., *Church Dogmatics*, Vol. I, Part 2, 280–361.

he had not in his miraculous condescension stepped forth towards us out of his utter hiddenness, men could have known nothing whatever about him. Religion is the vain attempt of self-righteous men to erect their own truth, to justify themselves by their own works, their own piety and their own pretension to discover God without the aid of divine grace. As such it is sinful unbelief. Barth's attitude towards religion can be understood only in the light of his total reaction against the kind of Liberal Protestant theology which had been dominant in Germany before the first world war.[1] Christianity, he declared, was not one religion among others; indeed, Christian faith was not a religion at all and could not be compared with the ethnic religions; it could only be contrasted with them. It was based upon God's revelation of himself, not upon man's anxieties, frustrated imaginings, feelings of self-importance or experiences of supernatural phenomena. Because it is attested by God's own word, it is true absolutely. Because even the faith by which it is confessed to be true is itself the free gift of God, it contains no element of human discovery and is incapable of being proved or disproved by human reasoning. Because it imparts the grace by which men's works can become acceptable in God's sight, it does not rely upon human righteousness or piety or insight. All is of faith and faith is of God; nothing is of man, for man is fallen, sinful and blind. All the scrupulosities and pieties by which nominally Christian folk turn their faith into religion are an abomination in God's sight.

And so we come to the idea of 'religionless Christianity'.

[1] The leaders of the *religionsgeschichtliche Schule* ('the history of religion school'), such as W. Bousset, R. Reitzenstein, W. Heitmuller, A. von Harnack, etc., had assumed that all religions could be investigated by the same scientific method and that Christianity was merely one religion amongst the other religions of the world. They had thus created a pseudo-scientific comparative study of religion, which begged the question of the truth of one religion as against another.

Is Religion a Good Thing?

The concept arises directly out of the Barthian definition of Christian faith as the acceptance of the unadulterated Word of God[1] and of religion as the superstitious veneration of the conjectures and traditions of men. Dietrich Bonhoeffer, the young German theologian who died a martyr's death at the hands of the Nazis in April, 1945, has been widely quoted as the advocate of religionless Christianity.[2] Bonhoeffer was a follower of Barth, and, provided that we understand the peculiar Barthian conception of 'religion', what he is saying makes good sense. For Bonhoeffer 'religion' meant, not faith in Christ as the living Word of God, but inherited metaphysical notions expressed in formal propositions and combined with an individualistic piety which bore no relation to daily life in the secular world. Mankind, he said, had come of age and had no use whatever for this kind of religiosity, which had all too often been what the churches in Germany had been keeping alive.

'Religionless' Christianity

Bonhoeffer was indeed speaking a timely word to the withdrawn and pietistic German churches, which, following the traditional Lutheran attitude of not interfering in the affairs of the State and of public morality, had left themselves only a small circle of churchy activity and individualistic piety within which their life was confined. Bismarck, the man of blood and iron who created the modern military state, and Bethmann Hollweg, the German Chancellor who in 1914 was so distressed that Britain had gone to war for the sake of 'a scrap of paper', were typical

[1] For Barth's understanding of this phrase, see Alan Richardson, *The Bible in the Age of Science*, London and Philadelphia, 1961, 93–6.

[2] E.g. by Bishop J. A. T. Robinson, *Honest to God*, London and Philadelphia, 1963, 23, 36–9, 99–104, etc. The brief references to the theme in Bonhoeffer's own work will be found in *Letters and Papers from Prison*, London and New York, 1953; Fontana ed., 1959.

Bible-reading pietists and active supporters of the Inner Mission. During Bonhoeffer's last days in prison, it would appear from his fragmentary writings, he came to see that the combination of Lutheran otherworldliness and Barthian despair about this world had made Protestantism in Germany irrelevant in the spheres of industry and politics and powerless to check the rise of Nazism or to contribute to the solution of the problems of a post-war Europe. Christians, he prophesied, would cease to be religious (i.e., interested only in churchy affairs and in individual salvation); they must become secular men, having broken out of their self-centred pietism and living in the secular world as 'men for others': to be a Christian was not to be religious but to be fully human.

In Britain (and in America) the dichotomy between the religious and the secular had never been so marked as it was in Germany. At the outbreak of the Kaiser's war the German government under Bethmann Hollweg was unquestionably the most devout in Europe, while the British cabinet, led by the sceptical Asquith, was probably the most irreligious. In the period between the two world wars the dominant Barthian theology did nothing to help traditional Lutheran pietism to come to grips with the realities of secular social and political life in Germany. But in the same period in Britain, America and other lands, such leaders as William Temple, J. H. Oldham, Charles Raven and the Niebuhrs—to mention only a few—aroused the churches to a lively sense of their political and social responsibilities.[1] To quote Professor Calhoun of Yale from a book published thirty years ago: 'A secularized, self-centred daily life on the one hand, and formalized pious occasions on the other, become scarred fragments which neither taken separately

[1] See esp. *The Churches survey their Task: the Report of the Conference at Oxford, July, 1937, on Church, Community and State*, with introduction by J. H. Oldham, London, 1937.

nor added together can be a living whole.'[1] 'Formalized pious occasions', which are what Bonhoeffer would have classed as 'religion', have indeed little to do either with the secular world or with Bonhoeffer's God who 'allows himself to be edged out of the world and on to the cross'.

When we have understood the difference between the religious situation in Germany between the wars and that of the English-speaking world, it is obvious that it is misleading to translate *religionslos* by 'religionless'. Much confusion would have been avoided if some such word as 'unpietistic' or 'unchurchy' had been employed. The Barthian usage of 'religion' is totally unfamiliar to those who speak the English language. Over the centuries the Latin word *religio* has been christianized and no longer means for us what it meant to pagan Romans or to early Christians. When, for instance, Francis Bacon said that 'a little philosophy inclineth men's minds to atheism, but depth in philosophy bringeth men's minds about to religion',[2] he meant the Christian religion, which he did not distinguish, as Barth does, from Christian faith. When the Book of Common Prayer speaks of 'the fellowship of Christ's religion' or beseeches God to 'increase in us true religion',[3] it is employing a usage which was firmly established centuries ago and which is ineradicable today. It is small wonder that good Christian folk are perplexed and distressed when they hear high ecclesiastics telling them that they should be religionless and that men come of age can have no use for religion.

The Biblical Attack upon Religion

The truth is that the Latin word *religio* has undergone a profound change of meaning since ancient times. It origi-

---

[1] R. L. Calhoun, *God and the Common Life*, New York, 1935, 12.
[2] *Essays*, 16; Atheism.   [3] Collects of Easter III and Trinity IV.

nally meant reverence for the gods, the prudential rendering to them of their dues, or just simply superstition. The attitude of the Roman world towards religion is aptly summed up in Edward Gibbon's famous epigram: 'The various modes of worship, which prevailed in the Roman world, were all considered by the people as equally true; by the philosopher, as equally false; and by the magistrate as equally useful.'[1] Indeed it would probably not be far wrong to say that this verdict is still valid in our own civilization. The unthinking populace still seems to suppose that all religions are equally true. One often hears the remark that 'we are all going the same way anyhow' and what does it matter whether we are Presbyterians or Anglicans or Methodists: and indeed, since we are all broad-minded nowadays, what does it matter whether we call God 'Father', or Allah, or Brahma, or the Ground of Being—we are all acknowledging a sort of something. And the rationalist philosophers are still with us to object that all religions are equally false, a proposition which is only formally different from saying that they are all equally true. As for the magistrates, in the broad sense of those responsible for the orderly running of the welfare state and for keeping the wheels of industry turning smoothly, they realize the importance of providing bread and circuses in honour of the local gods and of the goddess of Luck: absenteeism, we are told, always increases after the local gods have gone down before the visiting rival supermen on a Saturday afternoon, when the goddess of Luck has not smiled upon the home team. No British government dares to clap a capital-gains tax upon winnings in the football pools. Even so, Fortuna, who had for so long smiled upon Rome, at last withdrew her favour, having taken offence at the desertion of her shrines and games as a result of so many conversions to Christianity; and Rome was sacked by Alaric the Goth in AD 410.

[1] *Decline and Fall of the Roman Empire*, ch. 2.

Is Religion a Good Thing?

It should not surprise us to find that the early Christians did not think of their Way in terms of religion, or of God as one member of a class of gods. The pagan gods were lucky talismans, and such veneration as they attracted was little more than superstition—a perfectly valid rendering of *religio* in many contexts. Even the State religious observances on the 'holidays' were now only coldly formal ceremonies, and their social utility as a means of creating Imperial enthusiasm had to be supplemented by the introduction of Emperor worship. As the 'established' religion lost its hold, increasing numbers of people were attracted to the so-called 'mystery religions', a kind of warmly emotional evangelical nonconformity,[1] which offered individual salvation through initiation ceremonies of magical formulae and secret ritual behind locked doors. Such was the condition of religion when the Christian preachers first came forth out of Palestine into the Graeco-Roman world. No compromise with the mystery cults was tolerable, for they were but the relics of the oriental nature religions, against contamination with which the Old Testament prophets had for so long struggled to preserve the pure worship of Jehovah. The God of Israel, who now had made himself known to the world through Jesus Christ, was not one god amongst the 'gods many and lords many' of pagan religion. He was the 'jealous' God, who would 'very much object to being represented as a strong imperious person like Jupiter, or a frail beauty like Venus, or a delightful dandy like Apollo, or brute strength like Hercules, or a sportswoman like Diana, or a matron like Juno, or a whimsical mystery like the Sphinx'.[2] God was not *a* god, and the way of Christ was not *a* religion. The pagan people and the magistrates alike recognized this, because the principal

[1] Cf. N. P. Williams in *Essays Catholic and Critical*, ed. E. G. Selwyn, 3rd ed., London, 1929, 386.
[2] Father Andrew, SDC, *The Adventure of Prayer*, London, 1928, 31.

23

crime of which the Christians were accused was that of atheism: the Christians would not attend the sacred games of the Imperial and civic cults, nor would they drop incense upon the flame which burnt before the statue of the Emperor. Local patriotism, popular superstition and the super-imposed official cultus of imperial Rome were all affronted by this new and virulent form of atheism, which must inevitably bring down the wrath of the gods upon those who let it go unpunished. If the Christians of the first century had been asked whether religion was a good thing, they would have answered with a decisive negative.

In so answering their attitude would have been in accord with that of the Bible as a whole. Because over the centuries the word 'religion' has been Christianized, it doubtless comes as a surprise to many people today to discover that it is hardly a biblical word at all. It occurs nowhere in the English versions of the Old Testament, and it is rare in the New Testament.[1] The Greek word *deisidaimonia*, veneration of the supernatural, was, like its Latin equivalent, *religio*, nicely ambiguous; it occurs only twice in the New Testament (once adjectivally). St Paul could use it in a complimentary sense when he addressed the philosophers on Mars Hill: 'Ye men of Athens, I perceive that you are somewhat religious' (Acts 17.22, RV margin). On the other hand, Festus speaks with the cynical contempt of the Roman official for the strange customs of the subject races when he explains to Herod Agrippa the nature of the charges which the Jews had brought against Paul: 'They had certain questions against him of their own *deisidaimonia*' (Acts

---

[1] Apart from the two occurrences of *deisidaimonia* discussed in the text, we find Gal. 1.13f., where the Greek simply says 'Judaism'; Acts 26.5 and James 1.26f., where *threskeia* is used, properly meaning 'cultus'. St James is merely repeating what the Old Testament prophets had said so often, that good works are the only form of cult which God requires. These are all the occurrences of 'religion' in the English versions of the New Testament.

25.19)—'their peculiar superstition'. Festus is treating Agrippa as a man of the world like himself, who would approve of religion as a means of keeping the populace contented with their lot, but would resent the manner in which these intolerant Jews were always quarrelling about it as if it were something that really mattered. Pilate and Felix and Festus, and the other Roman magistrates, regarded religion as the opium of the people centuries before Karl Marx.

Of course, the attitude of the New Testament towards religion is only the continuation into the Hellenistic age of the struggle of the Old Testament prophets against the pagan religion of the peoples and tribes which surrounded Israel in Canaan. For the prophets, Jehovah was not a god amongst other gods, like the gods of Assyria or Babylon: he was the righteous God, and beside him there was no other. The gods of the Gentiles were idols, the work of men's hands; it was not these imaginary divinities who had brought the Philistines from Caphtor or the Syrians from Kir, as well as Israel from Egypt (Amos 9.7). They had not made the Pleiades and Orion (5.8) or stretched out the heavens like a curtain (Isa. 40.22). Bel and Marduk and Nebo were idols, powerless to save (Isa. 46.1f.); it was Jehovah alone who had raised up Assyria as the scourge of the unrighteous nations (Isa. 10.5f.) and had anointed Cyrus the Persian as the instrument of Israel's restoration (Isa. 45.1). God was the God of history and of nature as well. The immoralities of the fertility cults, the worship of the local baals of nature religion, were constant temptations to Israel in Canaan to forsake the stern and pure worship of the Holy God; a seductive whore beckoned from every high place and sacred grove to tempt a people, prosperous and relaxed in times of prosperity, towards the superstitious veneration of the gods of luck and luxury. Against all such trafficking with the fertility-baals the prophets thundered:

25

God was a jealous God, who would not share his honour with any national or local deities. In this sense the Old Testament as a whole can be described as one long, sustained assault upon religion. The worship of Jehovah was not *one* of the religions of the Fertile Crescent. It implied the abolition of religion as the ancient world understood it. There was one God only, and he had revealed his name to Israel.

The Christianizing of Religion

A case can thus be made out from the biblical attitude for Karl Barth's affirmation of Christianity as the abolition of religion. But such a case would have to ignore, as Barth does, the centuries of development during which the impact of Christianity has altered the very content and conception of religion itself in many parts of the world. Something more serious than a mere linguistic confusion in the use of the word remains to be cleared up. Barth had failed to notice that all human activity, including even religion, can be redeemed by the grace of God, whatever the depth of error and degradation that can be reached when grace is despised.[1] It is a matter of historical fact that Christianity has taken many of the institutions of pagan religion and transformed them into significant symbols of the truth of the Gospel. Barth himself writes movingly of the revelation of Christ under the heading of 'the Miracle of Christmas'.[2] He might have reflected upon the wisdom of the ancient Church, which did not try to stamp out the longing for new birth expressed in the age-old pagan festivals of the winter solstice, but converted the Roman feast of Sol Invicta, the unconquerable sun, into the yearly rejoicing over the birth of the

[1] It should be noted that Barth in his maturity has to some extent relented and become more hopeful about human achievements; see his *The Humanity of God*, Richmond, Virginia, 1960; London, 1962.
[2] *Church Dogmatics*, Eng. trans., Vol. I, Part 2.

Sun of Righteousness, the true light which lightens every man, the Saviour of the world and the desire of all nations. The relation between Christ's revelation and the religions of mankind cannot be one of total discontinuity, but is one of clear light as contrasted with partial seeing. Provided that we do not fall into the error of supposing that all religions are equally true, or of minimizing the very great differences between biblical religion and all other religions (as the *religionsgeschichtliche* school did), no great harm will be done by speaking of the Christian religion, and a more adequate historical understanding will be attained.

Perhaps we are now in a position to offer a definition of the *Christian* religion from the sociological and historical point of view. This will be a definition useful from the standpoint of academic study, though it will not be wholly adequate from that of the Christian believer himself. As we have remarked, no definitions are totally adequate, but are useful only from the viewpoint of a particular interest. Historically, then, we might say that the Christian religion results from the satisfaction of the human need of salvation from the condition in which men are born, from the oppressiveness of time and fate, by means of the proclamation of the revelation of God in Christ. Christianity is the only one of the world's religions to have become in any real sense universal, but opinions will vary about how far its success in helping peoples of many different lands and cultures to adjust their lives to reality is an index to the measure of truth which it contains. In any case, the history of Christianity, like the earthly life of its Founder, is not a success story.

It is improbable that Barth's attitude to religion will find acceptance within the ecumenical Christendom of the future, and it is therefore doubtful whether talk about religionless Christianity will long survive. The question will be answered outside Europeanized Christianity, whether Christian faith involves the abolition of religion or whether it completes and fulfils the insights and aspirations of men of every time and place, as they search for value, permanence and meaning in human life. This question was raised in an interesting and acute form at the New Delhi Conference of 1961,[1] but as a result of the supposed necessity of producing an 'agreed' statement, the discussion of it has been virtually eliminated from the official Report. Delegates from the churches of the East and of Africa argued from the Bible (against a strong array of Barth's followers from Europe) that just as God was the God of the whole world, not only of Israel, and that just as Christ was the Saviour of the *world*, not only of the Church, so also the eternal Word of God was the light which lightens every man, not only Christians. The light of the eternal Word has shone upon all those who, whether in ancient Greece or through India's long history, have in any way felt after truth and beauty and goodness, for it is he who in every age and every civilization puts into men's minds good desires. The Christian missionaries did not bring Christ to India: they found him there. 'Before Buddha was, I am.' All that the missionaries could do was what St Paul did in Athens and declare: 'What you worship in ignorance, this we set forth unto you.' During the coming decades, when it is likely that the advance of secularism will make further inroads into all the higher religions of the world, it is especially important that the dialogue with these other religions should be conducted from the Christian side on the basis of a sound interpretation of the biblical and Christian history. And this means, among other things, that we must go on beyond the point which we have thus far reached and formulate a genuinely biblical and Christian definition of 'religion'.

[1] Cf. *The New Delhi Report*, The Third Assembly of the World Council of Churches, ed. W. A. Visser 't Hooft, London and New York, 1962, 77f., 91f.

Is Religion a Good Thing?

SUGGESTIONS FOR FURTHER READING

Daniel T. Jenkins, *Beyond Religion: Truth and Error in 'Religionless Christianity'*, London and Philadelphia, 1962.

John Godsey, *The Theology of Dietrich Bonhoeffer*, Philadelphia and London, 1960.

Martin E. Marty (ed.), *The Place of Bonhoeffer*, New York and London, 1963.

Karl Barth, *The Humanity of God*, Richmond, Va., 1960; London, 1962.

David L. Edwards (ed.), *Honest to God and the Debate* (in one volume), London, 1963.

Hugo A. Meynell, *Sense, Nonsense and Christianity* (Stagbooks), London, 1964.

2

RELIGION AS THE ABOLITION
OF THE SECULAR

WE are still looking for a definition of 'religion' which shall be adequate from the point of view of a Christian who desires to take his stand on the ground of the Bible. We have already noted that outside those sciences which can employ mathematical measurement there are no totally adequate definitions; any definition of 'religion' will be adequate only from the standpoint of a particular approach or interest, such as that of the anthropologist or the social historian. The Buddhist, the Marxist and the Christian will each inevitably have his own definition of religion, and each of us must judge it in the light of his own experience and conviction. We are here concerned with the biblical-Christian definition. We have remarked that 'religion' is hardly a biblical word at all, but that during the course of the Christian centuries it has passed into the vocabulary of the Church and indeed has become domiciled in the English language. Our question therefore is: What is the proper use of the word 'religion' if we have respect to the biblical teaching?

The Christian Definition of Religion

What distinguishes the Christian understanding of religion from non-biblical attitudes is that it sees God rather than man as the primary agent in all religious activity. It is so 'natural' for man, being self-centred, to think of religion as something which men do; nevertheless such a view, though widespread, is an illusion, a distortion of the real state of affairs which arises from his false perspective. It was natural for Aristotle to reject the heliocentric view of the universe, because man is so obviously the centre of the world and everything must go round him. But just as at length Copernicus dethroned man from his central position in the universe, so too the Bible, centuries earlier, had dethroned man from his position of eminence as over against God. By magic man had presumed to bring the divine powers under his own control. Ancient religion had from time immemorial asserted that the king was God; by the most radical act of demythologizing in the history of thought, the Hebrews turned this assertion round and proclaimed that God is King. It was not man who should build a tower to heaven, but God who condescended to visit the sons of men on earth. From the opening chapters of Genesis onwards it is God, not man, who takes the initiative. If there has been an encounter between God and man, it took place because God came 'down' to where man was, not because man was clever enough to find out God (cf. Job 11.7) or strong enough to climb up to God's dwelling-place (Gen. 11.1-9).

Throughout the Bible God is represented as going forth to seek for man. The picture of God as the Shepherd-Ruler who goes forth to seek and to save that which was lost does not appear for the first time in the New Testament; it is found again and again in the Old Testament as one of the perennial images of the relationship between Jehovah and his people. It is not the sheep that set out to find the shepherd. Israel goes astray like a sheep that is lost (Ps. 119.176; Isa. 53.6), but Jehovah rules and corrects as well as feeds and protects his people (Ps. 23, etc.). Always in the Bible the encounter between God and man occurs as the result of the divine initiative. It is God who makes the approach and man who turns away. The God of the Bible is a God of seeking and sending; he addresses his people by the prophets whom he sends to them: 'Since the day that your fathers came forth out of the land of Egypt, I have sent unto you all my servants the prophets, daily rising up early and sending them . . . ' (Jer. 7.25). It is surely unnecessary to stress any further the truth that the Bible from cover to cover represents God as the one who searches for man and man as the one who hides himself from God (cf. Gen. 3.8-10). If there has been a meeting, it is because God has found man, not because man has discovered God. If there has been a choosing, it is God who has done the choosing: 'Ye have not chosen me, but I have chosen you' (John 15.16).

All this implies a reversal of our 'natural' and naturalistic judgments about religion as being primarily something which we do or think or feel. Religion *feels* like our quest for God or for reality, for truth and beauty and goodness. But the appearance is deceptive. From the biblical point of view human religious activity in all its forms, pagan as well as Christian, is man's response to something which God does. Because humanistic thinking does not start from God, it never gets to God; there is no way from man to God, only a way from God to man. Religion feels like our search for God, and humanistic thinkers, starting from this assumption, have even falsified the historical Gospels by representing Jesus as the great pioneer of the human enterprise in the search for God and his righteousness. Such humanism, as Dr John Baillie has pointed out in a telling passage, 'has often shown itself willing to place him in the vanguard of our human progress, to regard him as the spearhead of our human assault upon the unknown. He is, it is said, the great Trail-finder, the great Discoverer, our Leader in the forward march. In him humanity has attained.' But, Dr Baillie continues, 'if no more than this can be affirmed, then the whole glory has departed from the Christian religion. For this is neither what Christ believed about himself nor what Christians have ever believed about him. . . . The Christian Gospel is that God *sent* his Son into our history to be just what he was and to do just what he did. Christ is set forth as the spearhead not of human but of divine enterprise; and he is set in the vanguard not only of the human quest for God but also of God's great quest for the human heart.'[1] The mission of Christ, to seek and to save that which was lost, is but the historical manifestation of the enduring attitude and activity of God at all times and in all places. In the light of this teaching of the Gospels and of the whole Bible it is clear that from the Christian point of view religion must be defined, not as man's search for God, but as God's search for man. The controlling image of God, in the Christian way of looking at things, must remain the biblical picture of the Good Shepherd, and it is nonsense to say that this image formulated in a pastoral society cannot be understood in an industrial age.

The Non-Christian Religions

The Christian definition of religion as the human response to the divine initiative cannot be true only of the biblically based religions: it must be true also of all the religions of the world. Barth's early error of dismissing all 'religion' as a purely human and godless activity arose from his uncritical acceptance of the humanistic conception of religion as man's search for ultimate value and meaning in life. Of course, religious man is engaged on such a quest, but if we do not add something else, we shall have missed the heart of the matter. The something else is that God himself is the author and prompter of man's search for him, or for truth and meaning. There are no godless searchers for truth and value, because the very fact that they are engaged upon such

[1] *Invitation to Pilgrimage*, Oxford and New York, 1942, 84.

a pursuit means that they have not been left alone by God. God is the origin as well as the goal of the quest, the first step as well as the last, the Alpha as well as the Omega. If we might adapt the great saying of Pascal,[1] even the most doubt-beset enquirer might take comfort from the fact that he could not have begun his search if God had not been present with him, prompting him. Whatever at the beginning of our search we might mean by God, the word must in some way be associated in our minds with the object of the quest for truth and beauty and goodness. These things were not of our creation, for then we would already possess them; our incipient knowledge of them is given to us that we might desire them in the fullness of their source and home; or, as the biblical writer declared, 'We love because he first loved us' (I John 4.19).

The divine quest for man finds its response in every religion of the world. As St Paul said to the Athenians, 'he created every race of men of one stock, to inhabit the whole earth's surface. He fixed the epochs of their history and the limits of their territory. They were to seek God, and, it might be, touch and find him; though indeed he is not far from each one of us' (Acts 17.26f., NEB). God is not more interested in Europeans and their religious institutions than he is in Africans or Chinese and their religious aspirations. He is equally the Lord of all and wills all men to come to the knowledge of his truth. This does not mean that all religions are equally true, for some have clearly attained more worthy conceptions of God than others. Some, indeed, have perverted the wholesome longings which prompted them to search for God; corrupt practices have often been associated with religion, as the history of Christianity itself shows. It is all too true that, as St Paul has said (Rom. 1.21-3), men knowing God have refused to honour him as God and their misguided minds have been plunged in darkness. We all

[1] *Pensées,* vii. 553.

know that in every continent pure religion has too often compromised its integrity by allowing itself to become the instrument of the very humanistic religion of nationalism. Many such charges could be brought against religion in all its forms, but the spirit and essence of religion are not to be confounded with its perversion. Before the Gospel of Christ had ever been preached amongst them, men in many lands had responded to the divine initiative and had expressed their understanding of the eternal truth in various noble forms. Before the word of God became incarnate in Christ, the word of God was already present in all the world: 'the light was in being, light absolute, enlightening every man born into the world'.[1] The word of God was indeed present and at work in India from the beginning, long before the Christian missionaries set foot there.

The situation of India, after all, is no different from that of any other country to which the Gospel has come: it happened in former centuries in Greece, or North Africa, or Europe. In a well-known passage St Augustine describes how, before his conversion to Christ, he had learnt from the pagan philosophers of the ancient world (he is thinking chiefly of the Platonists and Stoics) many truths about God which are contained in the prologue to the Fourth Gospel—that the eternal word (*logos*) was in the beginning with God, that man's soul is not itself the light but bears witness to the light amidst the surrounding darkness which cannot overcome it, and that the word of God is the true light which illuminates every man coming into the world.[2] He also states succinctly what it was that the preachers of the Gospel carried to the wise men of the nations, the vital truth which he did not find in the writings of the philosophers: 'that the word was made flesh and dwelt among us I did not read there'. This is the good news which at the same time cor-

[1] The marginal translation in *The New English Bible* of John 1.9.
[2] *Confessions*, VII, 9.

35

roborates, corrects and transcends the conjectures and gropings of the searchers after truth of all the nations. It does not cancel but fulfils the insights into truth which the religions of the world have attained, as they have responded to the promptings of the God who seeks to draw all men to himself. An older generation of missionaries in the nineteenth century was wrong, theologically and strategically, in excoriating all the religious ideas and practices of the non-Christian world as 'heathen abominations' and in imagining that the perversions of the ancient religions were to be identified with their essence.[1] Today the shoe is often on the other foot, when many students and immigrants from the emergent nations so easily identify the apparent formalism and coldness of our British church life with the essential core of Christianity. The dialogue between Christians and men of other religions, so urgently needed today in face of the rising challenge of secularism, must be conducted out of the knowledge of each religion at its best, since parodies of religion merely supply its enemies with ammunition, and the scoring of debating points leads no one into the way of truth. If the social anthropologists are right in suggesting that the phenomenon of religion arises out of the universal human dissatisfaction with the condition into which men are born, then men of all religions are involved in a common predicament and would do well to face it together. Christians, who believe that God is not far from each one of us, should expect to discover in every religious aspiration traces of that word without whom nothing was made that has been made.

Secular Christianity

If the definition of religion as man's response to the divine initiative is accepted, then any conception of a 'secular'

[1] Cf. M. A. C. Warren's penetrating analysis of the missionary task of the Church in his *The Missionary Movement from Britain in Modern History*, London, 1965, esp. chaps. 5 and 6.

sphere in which God is not present and active becomes
unthinkable for Christians. Before we ask what is meant by
'secular Christianity', it would be wise to examine the word
'secular' more closely. The Latin *saeculum* meant an age,
perhaps a century or more (cf. in church Latin, *in saecula
saeculorum*, 'for ever and ever'). *Saecularis* meant 'belonging
to a particular age': the 'secular games', for instance, were
celebrated at an interval of a hundred and twenty years, and
the appropriate 'secular hymns' were sung at them, for the
games were religious occasions. It was in the Middle Ages
that the first step was taken towards separating the secular
from the religious sphere, when 'secular' came to be used
in the sense of 'pertaining to this present age' as contrasted
with the things concerned with the age to come (cf. 'the
secular arm', or 'secular clergy' as contrasted with the
'religious' or 'regular clergy' who lived according to the rule,
regula, of their order). The civil sphere gradually achieved
independence from ecclesiastical control or supervision,
and after the period of the Reformation many areas of life
became increasingly autonomous in this sense. By the nineteenth century the secular was often thought of as the sphere
in which neither the Church nor the Christian conscience
had any right or qualification to interfere (e.g., politics,
business, science, etc.). We find preachers like Robertson of
Brighton denouncing the development: 'we stigmatize first
one department of life and then another as secular, and so
religion becomes a pale, unreal thing.'[1] In the twentieth
century, when many more 'departments of life' (e.g., the
universities, education in general, the social services, the
hospitals) have been added to the 'secular' sphere, religion
might seem to have become almost entirely confined to the
narrow area of ecclesiastical activity and personal piety, and
thus an even paler and less real thing. In the face of this
continual narrowing down of the sphere of the religious one

[1] *Sermons*, IV, ii, 20; 1863.

may sympathize with those who speak of secular Christianity: Christians should stop being pietistic and should actively concern themselves with the affairs of secular life. They must live in the world as 'men for others'; to be a Christian, as Bonhoeffer said, is not to be churchy but to be fully human. To teach that Christian responsibility extends far beyond the sphere of church services and organization has been the constant endeavour of Christian leaders from the writing of the New Testament epistles to the printing of the *New Delhi Report*.

If this is what is meant by 'secular Christianity', nothing more than a verbal objection need be taken to the phrase; it certainly emphasizes one very important aspect of New Testament faith and practice. We would have preferred to speak of the object of Christian religion as the abolition of the secular sphere, so that no 'departments of life' should be thought of as outside the sovereign lordship of Christ; this would have been a way of stating the matter more in accordance with the New Testament's own attitude towards 'the world'. The secular kingdoms are destined to become the kingdom of our Lord and his Christ (Rev. 11.15), and Jesus in the Fourth Gospel declares that his kingdom is not secular and that his servants do not join issue in secular disputes (John 18.36). A continual reiteration of the word 'secular' obscures the finely balanced New Testament distinction between being in the world and yet not being of the world (cf. John 17.14-18): Christians have in their faith a standing-ground above and beyond this-worldly concerns and they cannot be wholly absorbed in the world as *merely* secular men. There are, however, amongst the contemporary advocates of secular Christianity those who deny that there is any transcendent standing-ground in faith from which Christians may exercise a genuinely radical discrimination in secular affairs.[1]

[1] Professor R. Gregor Smith does not do this in his *Secular Christianity*.

Thus, the American theologian Paul van Buren tells us that secularism involves 'concern for men, convictions that life is worth living in a certain way, and a high valuation on human relationships'.[1] Secularism, he says, is compatible with complete agnosticism about a transcendental realm or about the existence of God, since such notions are meaningless to secular men, deeply affected as they are by empiricist attitudes. 'We are saying that it is possible today to be agnostic about "otherworldly" powers and beings, but that people matter.'[2] The historic Christian faith, which van Buren discards, was able to give a rational account of *why* people matter; it affirmed, quite simply, that people matter because God loves them (cf. Rom. 14.15; I John 3.16f.; 4.19-21). But van Buren's secular Christians have no need of the grace of God; they will choose to live by the ethics and example of Jesus. Yet they have been laid hold of by something: they have been grasped by the history of Jesus, and this means the Risen Jesus, for the Gospel which lays hold of secular Christians is the Easter proclamation itself. We are left in complete mystification why this positive Christology should be denied any theological implications; the meaning of the Gospel, we are told, is secular because it lies in areas of the historical and the ethical, not in the meta-

---

(London, 1966). Unfortunately his book appeared after this one had gone to press. In the last section he has much to say about 'secularism' which is profound and helpful, though his use of the word is confusing. In particular, his clarification of the meaning of Bonhoeffer's enigmatic last words is illuminating. The first two sections (on Faith and History) are probably the clearest exposition of the theology of Bultmann in the English language. The bifurcation of history into *Geschichte* and *Historie* is adopted as self-evident, despite the reaction in contemporary historiography from Enlightenment positivism, the consequences of which for theology are discussed in the present writer's *History Sacred and Profane* (London and Philadelphia, 1964). The only reference to the latter work (pp. 75f.) would seem to indicate that his acquaintance with it is superficial.

[1] *The Secular Meaning of the Gospel*, New York and London, 1963, 194.
[2] Ibid., 195.

physical or the religious.[1] It is even argued that this is what the Chalcedonian Fathers really meant to say and what they would have said if they had had a twentieth-century education. It could be more plausibly argued that this is what the Arians would have said, because a Christ who is not of one substance with the Father reveals to us nothing of ultimate being. Van Buren's secular Gospel tells us nothing about a Christ who has come forth from the Father, and so (in Dr Baillie's phrase) 'the whole glory has departed from the Christian religion'.

Secularism

One good reason for avoiding the phrase 'secular Christianity' is that it might be taken to imply the advocacy of a humanistic Jesusology of the van Buren type, or what he calls 'secularism', the assertion that 'God' is only a symbol and that 'loving God' is only another way of saying loving one's neighbour.[2] But there is another reason for avoiding the word 'secularism' in any connection with the Gospel of Christ: it cannot now be divested of its original connotation. It was in 1851 that it first made its appearance. It seems to have been coined by G. J. Holyoake (1817-1906) as the name for his philosophical and ethical system, which sought to interpret and order life without recourse to belief in God, the Bible or a future life. He set up Secular Societies in several English towns; and as a result of their activities the word 'secular' became identified in many minds with 'secularist'. The redoubtable Charles Bradlaugh, who was president of the London Secular Society from 1858 to 1890, made history by demonstrating that an 'atheist' (though probably he was better described as an agnostic) could sit as a Member of Parliament without taking the oath. The Secularists undoubtedly sponsored many socially progres-

---

[1] Ibid., 197.   [2] Ibid., 182f.

sive causes and worked hard for the betterment of the condition of the labouring classes at a time when many conventionally religious people were indifferent or even hostile to reform; but their bitter anti-religious propaganda and their hatred of Christianity has left an unpleasant hangover in the English mind. Perhaps the word 'secularism' does not awaken echoes of 'old, unhappy, far-off things and battles long ago' in the American mind. However that may be, the successors of the Secularists of yesterday have abandoned the word and nowadays prefer to call themselves 'humanists'.[1] It would help to remove some of the confusion in contemporary religious discussion if theologians would follow their example and abandon the use of the words 'secular' and 'secularism' in view of their association with an unhappy era of anti-religious propaganda.[2]

In actual English usage today the word 'secularism' commonly denotes the widespread practical tendency to ignore God and all religious questions and observances through preoccupation with this-worldly ('secular') concerns, keeping up with 'everyone else', 'getting on' in the world, the 'rat-race' which leaves one too exhilarated or too exhausted to sit down and think about ultimate things. It is not the honest and serious theories of the old-fashioned

[1] Thus, the Rationalist Press Association, the instrument of organized humanism, publishes *The Humanist*, incorporating the secularist *Literary Guide* and *Rationalist Review* of former days. Of course, 'humanism', properly meaning an education based on the classics, represented a splendid development of late mediaeval and Renaissance Christian civilization (cf. the humanists Erasmus, Colet and More), and Christians are not prepared to surrender the word. Its present usage by latter-day secularists, rationalists and agnostics can be traced back to Auguste Comte's use of it in connection with his 'religion of humanity' and is barely a hundred years old.

[2] If, as seems probable, the word 'secular' has crept into theological usage as a rough equivalent of Bonhoeffer's *religionslos* (secular Christianity = religionless Christianity), then its presence is due to Barth's seminal error of regarding religion as something which man does and not as his response to the divine activity in the world.

secularists or present-day 'humanists' which constitute a danger to religious conviction, but the practical worldliness of the millions for whom the technological revolution has opened up hitherto undreamed-of possibilities of affluence, at least for those who belong to social groups strong enough to fight for their 'rights'. The Utopian ideology of the unauthentic masses, surely as disquieting to thoughtful humanists as it is to Christians, is a menace to the moral structures of society and therefore to society itself. It is hardly necessary to list the symptoms of the moral disintegration of Western civilization, for these are obvious to all: the absence of a sense of responsibility in the industrial order, the insatiable demands of almost all sections of the community for more money for less work, the boredom of aimlessness particularly among the young, the mounting crime statistics, drug addiction, suicides, broken homes, illegitimacy, venereal disease, gambling, and so on. These things constitute a challenge to all serious people, whether humanist or Christian, and the challenge is sharpened by Lord Devlin's reminder: 'No society has yet solved the problem of how to teach morality without religion.'[1]

Secularization

Secularization is not to be confused with secularism in either its original or its current sense. Secularization, which (as we have noted) has been going on since the high Middle Ages, is in itself neither good nor bad; it was inevitable. After the destruction of the Roman Empire by the invading barbarians, the Church was compelled to take control of the re-ordering of civilization, and thus inevitably came to wield great political and economic power. Power corrupts, and the Church did not remain uncorrupted by the exercise

[1] *The Enforcement of Morals*, London and New York, 1965, 25.

42

of power. With the rise of nationalism and under the stimulus of the Christian humanism of the Renaissance, European man 'came of age' and inevitably demanded and obtained freedom from clerical tutelage and all that this implied. The ensuing secularization of the various 'departments of life' did not necessarily imply the rejection of Christianity, though the danger of this was increased the longer the process of emancipation from ecclesiastical control was delayed. By the middle of the twentieth century the process has been more or less completed, though in different ways and in different degrees in the different national states which once constituted Christendom. In the period of nearly nine centuries since Gregory VII on his accession to the Papacy wrote to the 'nations' to remind them that from the days of St Peter the see of Rome had been their lord and master, or humbled the Holy Roman Emperor at Canossa, to the day when Pope Paul flew across the Atlantic to appeal to the United Nations in New York, the process of secularization has been completed. It is not to be deplored but accepted as the visible sign of the success of the civilizing mission of the Church.

It is wholly to the good that after centuries of Christian teaching it is now almost universally assumed that governments should accept responsibility for many works which were once the care of the Church. The State has the power, which the Church as an ecclesiastical institution could not and should not have, to provide through taxation what the uncoerced citizens would never pay for voluntarily. Over against the depressing miasma of practical secularism in our midst should be set the real gains of actualized Christian teaching, such as the acceptance by the State of responsibility for the education of the young, the financing of universities and research, the social services, the care of the sick, the aged and the mentally handicapped, or the provision of aid to underdeveloped countries. And if many 'humanists'—those who believe that 'people matter' or that 'loving God' is only another way of saying loving one's neighbour—find their fulfilment in social service, this, too, is something to be welcomed.[1] 'By their fruits ye shall know them.' There is still plenty of work for Christians to do inside as well as outside the State provision for welfare. Without the warmth which self-giving love can bring to the impersonal ministrations of the State-provided system, the latter will remain at best 'love in a cold climate'.

Secularization, as we have defined it, is not to be confused with practical secularism, and we should not blame the latter upon the former. There never was a time when the masses, even in the once Christian nations, were thoroughly Christianized, though until perhaps the seventeenth century the illusion of Christianization was engendered when the whole population was baptized in infancy by order of the government and dissent was punished by the magistrate. The Church's own failures are sufficient to account in large measure for the growth of practical secularism: the breaking up of the unity of the Church into several competing denominations; the reluctance of the various churches to relinquish ecclesiastical controls and to accept social changes; the intellectual timidity of many Christians in face of the revolution in scientific, historical and theological thinking; their absorption in the institutional and pietistic life of the withdrawn community—all these things must be included in any account of the growth of indifference to religious and moral issues amongst a considerable number of people in lands which were formerly reckoned as Christendom. Secularization may indeed have facilitated the process, but if it did so it was chiefly because the churches were reluctant to adapt themselves to the irreversible logic

[1] See Professor Paul Halmos's suggestive study of the 'faith' of psychiatrists, social case workers, etc., in *The Faith of the Counsellors*, London, 1965.

of change and therefore often missed the opportunities which the new situations had opened up for them.[1]

The Christian Presupposition of Secularization

The secularized world (as we have defined it) can be understood only as a development from Christian civilization. In the concluding chapter of his recent Gifford Lectures[2] the distinguished physicist Professor C. F. von Weizsäcker argues that the modern world can largely be understood as the result of a secularization of Christianity. His analysis of the situation is searching, and it is all the more suggestive because he looks at things through the eyes of an historically-minded scientist. We would have preferred to say that the modern world can be understood only as the result of the secularization of Christendom or of Christian civilization, rather than of Christianity.[3] One might even say that it can be understood only as the result of the acceptance by declericalized governments of those ideas and ideals which first found expression in the movements of thought and in the institutions of the high civilization of the Christian Middle Ages. The potential of these ideas and ideals could be realized only after the authoritarian and paternalistic restrictions of ecclesiastical supervision had been removed; and this is secularization. It was within the Christian civilization of Europe that the modern scientific movement and the humane tradition were born,

[1] The American Professor Harvey Cox, in his widely read book, *The Secular City: Secularization and Urbanization in Theological Perspective* (New York and London, 1965), seems to equate secularization with urban development and thus offers a different definition and therefore a different assessment from those suggested here. He provides much food for thought even for those who do not entirely agree with his analysis of the situation or his theological perspective.

[2] *The Relevance of Science*, London, 1964; New York, 1965, 157–82.

[3] Possibly there is a difficulty of translation here: the German word *Christentum* can mean either 'Christianity' or 'Christendom'.

from which in due course sprang modern science and technology, the critical spirit of free enquiry and academic liberty, and eventually the concept of self-government for whole peoples enjoying political responsibility on a basis of universal literacy. However far these things may still be from effective realization, there is no doubt that they are what the whole world desires. The vision of a world from which ignorance, hunger, drudgery and oppression have been banished has become at least a conceivable goal as a result of the development of modern science and technology, scientific medicine and agriculture; and these things, at one remove, are to be reckoned amongst the blessings of the Gospel of Christ.

The whole world desires these blessings, even where it is unaware of their origin and indifferent to the proclamation of the Gospel. It is rapidly becoming a secularized world, that is, a Europeanized world (however much it resents the 'colonialism' which initiated the movement towards world secularization). Governments, even in the newest nations, cannot too avidly build schools and universities and technical colleges, hospitals and agricultural institutes, and all the other institutions which are essential for progress in the sense of radical secularization. The Christian hope of a consummation in a life beyond this world (often explicitly rejected by the advocates of 'secular Christianity') has been clouded by dreams of unending progression towards universal leisure and affluence based upon the techniques, both technological and psychological, of a scientific civilization. A kingdom of Christ which is not of this world is irrelevant to the ideology thrown up by the processes of Westernization, which in our age have opened up the Orient and Africa and made conceivable the prospect of the secularized world-state of the future.

Christians and secular humanists will disagree over certain important questions which arise from these considerations.

Christians will regard the basic religious and moral insights which inspired the achievements of mediaeval Christendom as being of permanent validity and indispensable to the well-being of mankind, even in a world which has been necessarily and rightly secularized. Humanists will regard the religious development from biblical times to the rise and disintegration of Christendom as merely a stage on the road to the Enlightenment, a stage which has now been outgrown and of which the childish religious presuppositions can be left behind. But they will surely have much to say to each other, since they are likely to agree that moral considerations are of the utmost importance, and that the mindless ideology which informs what we have called practical secularism is the enemy of any kind of truly human progress. Christians, it is to be hoped, will not try to make apologetic ammunition out of the serious moral dilemmas of a secularized age; and humanists, one may likewise hope, will not concentrate their attack upon religion in all its forms as public enemy number one. The issues at stake are too momentous. Man's recently acquired mastery over nature will turn into a curse and not a blessing, unless he achieves some kind of moral mastery over his own evil propensities. The real disagreement between Christians and humanists does not lie in the area of shadow-boxing over the question of the existence of a metaphysical God, but in the very live issue of whether the inexorable demands of righteousness can be met out of human resources without the aid of an all-ruling and all-loving power by which the blessings of secularization have thus far been precariously attained and by which their promise for the future may in some measure be fulfilled. The Christian answer to this question involves the assertion that there are no 'departments of life' where the law and the grace of God do not operate and the consequent resolution to seek the abolition of secularism in both its theoretical and its practical forms.

SUGGESTIONS FOR FURTHER READING

John Baillie, *The Sense of the Presence of God*, Oxford and New York, 1962.

Martin Jarrett-Kerr, *The Secular Promise: Christian Presence amid Contemporary Humanism*, London and Philadelphia, 1964.

R. J. Hammer, *Japan's Religious Ferment: Christian Presence amid Faiths Old and New*, London and New York, 1961.

John V. Taylor, *The Primal Vision: Christian Presence amid African Religion*, London and Philadelphia, 1963.

M. A. C. Warren, *The Missionary Movement from Britain in Modern History*, London, 1965.

A. T. van Leeuwen, *Christianity in World History*, London, 1964; New York, 1965.

K. M. Baxter, *Speak What We Feel: A Christian Looks at the Contemporary Theatre*, London, 1964; Nashville, Tennessee, 1965 (under the title: *Contemporary Theatre and the Christian Faith*).

Alan Richardson, *University and Humanity*, London, 1964.

C.-F. von Weizsäcker, *The Relevance of Science: Creation and Cosmogony*, London, 1964; New York, 1965.

Harvey Cox, *The Secular City: Secularization and Urbanization in Theological Perspective*, New York and London, 1965.

P. Moore, *The Church Reclaims the City*, New York and London, 1964.

Kathleen Heasman, *Christians and Social Work*, London, 1965.

E. L. Mascall, *The Secularisation of Christianity*, London, 1965.

R. Gregor Smith, *Secular Christianity*, London, 1966.

3

VARIETIES OF RELIGIOUS ATHEISM

SOMETIMES today the question is asked whether men who live in an atheistic age can believe in God without changing themselves back into men of a pre-scientific age. Those who ask this question assume, quite correctly, that it is impossible for intelligent people today to revert to the supernaturalist metaphysical notions of the past: twentieth-century folk know that disease is caused by germs and not by demons and that the perturbations of Uranus are caused by Neptune and not by the finger of God. But they then go on to argue that modern men can no longer believe in a God 'up there' who controls the world from outside by means of supernatural agencies from a mythical transcendent realm. 'Our image of God must go', and in its place some philosophical concept must be found which can satisfy our deep human needs in the new religionless age. If it is true that, in spite of all the excellent theological teaching which has been printed and spoken during the present century, we still cling to the eighteenth-century deistic idea of God, then indeed our image of God must go; we must try to catch up with the theological revolution of the nineteenth century, before we decide to turn to philosophical speculation.

Speculative Religiosity

Three main types of philosophical belief are offered for our comfort after our image of God has gone. They cover several sub-varieties, ranging from the near-Christian to the positively anti-Christian, but we have space to consider only the main types. They are in conflict with one another, and perhaps the only way in which they could be bracketed together would be to say that they are all varieties of religious atheism. The first which we shall consider may be described as philosophical idealism, because, though highly syncretistic, it looks more like Hegel's metaphysics than anything else. It is represented by the 'System' of Paul Tillich,[1] which combines elements from almost every thinker, ancient and modern, eastern and western, in a great web of symbols and paradoxes. It is not taken seriously in Europe, although it would be generally admitted that in the seemingly limitless deserts of words there are pages which appear like oases of refreshment and sustenance for the weary traveller. We need not concern ourselves here with the philosophical criticism of the 'System'.[2] Theologically Tillich ceased to be interesting long ago. Probably the reason why he became so widely admired in America was that, because of the pervasive ambiguity of his language, it is possible to miss the true implication of what he is saying and to read one's own meanings into his words and thus to be hypnotized into finding comfort in oases which are only mirages.

All the great words of the Christian faith are 'reinterpreted'; everything is symbolic and nothing means what it used to mean before it was processed in the 'System'. For instance, there is a 'God beyond God', who is not the God of theism but a non-personal something called being-itself, from which there emanates a power of being which overcomes the threat of non-being. Salvation means deliverance, not from sin, evil and death, but from the dread of non-

[1] As set forth in his three massive volumes entitled *Systematic Theology*, the last of which appeared in 1963 (Chicago; London, 1964).
[2] For a sympathetic exposition and criticism from the philosophical point of view see *Paul Tillich: an Appraisal* by J. Heywood Thomas (London and Philadelphia, 1963); cf. also G. H. Tavard, *Paul Tillich and the Christian Message* (New York and London, 1962).

being. Faith is not belief in Christ's revelation of God but is 'the state of being grasped by the power of being-itself'. Justification by faith is replaced by 'the courage to be', the acceptance of acceptance which issues from participation in the power of being ('everything that is participates in the power of being'), the power beyond the God of theism, which emanates from the ground of being. The Church is not the community which was called into existence by the proclamation of the Gospel of Christ, but is an entity (composed, presumably, of Tillich's disciples) which stands for the power of being-itself, that is, the God who transcends the God of the religions; this 'church' mediates the courage to be.[1] The Christ is the New Being, which we may be sure has appeared in history, though we cannot be sure that his name is Jesus of Nazareth,[2] since all historical evidence concerning him is at best only faintly probable. Thus, all the great words of the Christian faith become symbols which stand for something other than their historical meaning: Incarnation, the Trinity, the Spirit, and so on. There is no closer connection between the Gospel of Christ and the 'System' of Tillich than there was between that Gospel and the various Gnostic 'systems' which appeared during the earlier centuries of Christian history.[3]

Whether Tillich's 'System', when it has been properly understood, can be said to be 'gospel', good news, in any sense at all, must remain an open question; certainly his sermon 'The Eternal Now'[4] seems to assert that there is no

[1] All these statements will be found in the last chapter of Tillich's *The Courage to Be*, 1952 (Fontana ed., 1962, 152–83).

[2] *Systematic Theology*, II, 114.

[3] Anyone who doubts this statement would do well to read Kenneth Hamilton, *The System and the Gospel*, London and New York, 1963.

[4] Printed in *The Eternal Now*, New York and London, 1963, 103–11. This sermon is a typical example of the way in which the constant biblical references and allusions make it possible to read Christian meanings into paragraphs which deny, though obscurely, the truths of the Christian proclamation.

life beyond our transient 'now', and we are left to find what comfort we can in exalted language about our 'return to the eternal ground of time' after having 'received a limited span of time as *our* time'. Tillich's fundamentally atheistic philosophy is concealed by his incurable religiosity, and nothing could better illustrate the confusion of some of those who seek to meet the needs of a religionless age than their admiration for one who has so diligently sought to translate secular philosophical theory into religious language.

Existentialism in an Atheistic Mode

Existentialism may be very broadly characterized as that kind of philosophy which looks towards our most inward human experience, rather than towards the knowledge accumulated by the natural sciences, as the source of our deepest understanding of existence. It rejects the assumption of positivism that scientific knowledge (after the manner of the natural sciences) is the only or the most important kind of knowledge,[1] and insists that meaning is found only in our own inwardness (subjectivity). Thus, existentialism is not in itself either Christian or anti-Christian, and there are Christian and non-Christian existentialists: Kierkegaard, who invented the word, and Marcel are Christian existentialist thinkers; Heidegger and Sartre are non-Christian existentialists. Our present concern is with the current vogue of theological existentialism which has grown out of Rudolf Bultmann's attempt to re-state the truth of the New Testament in terms of Heidegger's existentialist philosophy and so to make it intelligible to modern men. Bultmann was Professor of New Testament studies at Marburg from 1921

[1] This attitude is ably presented in Barbara Wootton's *Testament for Social Science*, London, 1950, and is half-consciously accepted by millions of folk in our modern secular society.

to 1951 and is now an octogenarian; we shall not be concerned so much with his theology as with that of his younger disciples and admirers who have pushed his speculations further than he was himself prepared to take them.[1]

Existentialist theologians have a horror of what they call 'objectivizing'. This means the externalizing of what are really our human mental states and giving them an objective status outside ourselves. In a pre-scientific culture this process goes on uninhibitedly. Those good influences or moral compulsions which flow in upon us from persons or social forces around us are objectivized as angels or good spirits, while all the evil pressures upon us are personified as demons or evil spirits. These are credited with an existence independent of ourselves, and so we get a heaven above us, populated by a hierarchy of angels and superhuman beings under the overall lordship of God, and beneath us an underworld of evil spirits who are the minions of the arch-enemy, Satan or the Devil. The earth becomes the battle-ground of the contending forces of good and evil. In the various Gnostic 'systems', which it is sometimes claimed (without any real historical evidence) were contemporary with St Paul, a Divine Man was alleged to have come down from heaven imparting to the initiates secret pass-words which would enable them after death to escape the planetary guardians of the gates of heaven and secure their admission into the world of light. Such, according to Bultmann, is the world-view of the New Testament, and its theology of Jesus as the Saviour-God from heaven is shaped by it. The whole mythological framework of the Gospels must be abandoned in order that men who today live in a scientific age may hear the authentic message of Jesus, unencumbered by magic,

[1] For Bultmann see the chapter on 'The Existentialist Theology' in Alan Richardson, *The Bible in the Age of Science*, London and Philadelphia, 1961, 100–21, and, at greater length, John Macquarrie, *An Existentialist Theology*, London and New York, 1955.

miracle and myth. The genuine word of God, of which Jesus was the bearer, challenges men in their inward existence to renounce their pretensions of self-sufficiency and all their fears of self-recognition and of death, and to become open to the future by the acceptance of the new kind of existence which the proclaimed message of Jesus, supremely realized in his own triumphant death, makes possible for them. The new understanding of existence brought by Jesus accomplishes a change in our existence itself, and this constitutes in us a new kind of authentic being.

This is as far as Bultmann was prepared to go, and it is indeed far enough; it leaves very little of the historical Christian faith, but at least it makes room for a genuine word of *God* to men. It was inevitable that others would go further. Why, it is asked, should we stop here? Why should we suppose that there is any revelation ('word') of God from outside ourselves? Is not the 'word of God', which the prophets proclaimed, only an exteriorization of their own deep human compulsion, suitably dressed up according to the usage of a pre-scientific age in a garb which invests their utterance with a supernatural sanction? And does the challenge of Jesus himself lose anything of its compelling power, if we moderns see him only as 'the man for others' who in virtue of his inherent moral authority commands our obedience? Can anything be added to it by clothing it with the obscuring verbiage of theology? Must not the consistent demythologizer go with Teutonic thoroughness to the end of the road, and regard even the existence of God as merely the ultimate objectivization of our inward human experiences? At this point we shall have reached an atheistic interpretation of the Bible and the Gospels. The objectivizing of certain basic experiences of our existence, which were personified as 'God' in a pre-scientific age, are no longer thought necessary for us in the space-age, when we are adult enough to recognize them for what they are and to put aside the comforting illusions of the childhood of the human race. Whatever else may be said about this point of view, it is at least obvious that it has ceased to be theologically interesting, for it acquiesces in the total capitulation of theology to philosophy. It puts an end to the Christian faith as a real relation with the God who has revealed himself in human history. It is a mark of the confusion of thought in our times that there should be men, who think of themselves as theologians, who are yet prepared to speak of God as nothing more than a symbol of our own self-understanding, or as a linguistic event by means of which we can speak of our own authentic existence. The phenomenon is not, however, novel; Helmut Gollwitzer quotes appositely a saying of Heine more than a century ago: 'In Germany it is the theologians who are making an end of the good God— *On n'est jamais trahi que par les siens.*'

There is a notable similarity between the conclusions of the more radical existentialists and those of Paul Tillich, although they have been reached by a different road. Herbert Braun, for instance, dissolves God into the constituents of our own self-understanding and claims that this is what the New Testament writers themselves really meant to say.[1] The 'existence' thus disclosed as transcending theism reminds us of Tillich's claim to have advanced beyond the God of theism; both Tillich and Braun, in their different ways, find God in the depth of our being. Braun in one of his essays boasts that he has succeeded in setting forth the message of the New Testament without using the word 'God' at all[2] though generally he does not seem to wish to avoid its use. Both Tillich and Braun make the mistake of identifying the biblical and Christian faith in God with theistic metaphysics, which is a quite inexcusable historical error.

[1] H. Braun, *Gesammelte Studien zum Neuen Testament und seiner Umwelt*, Tübingen, 1962, 243–309; cf. also Schubert M. Ogden, *Christ without Myth*, New York, 1961; London, 1962, 137.
[2] P. 297.

Whatever it was that called that faith into being, it was certainly not a process of philosophical reasoning which resulted in the adoption of metaphysical theism. The claim to have 'transcended' both theism and atheism is based upon a muddled confusion of the two in an unconvincing effort to have it, philosophically speaking, both ways. The Psalmist pronounces the verdict upon such vanity: 'He that sitteth in the heavens shall laugh; the Lord shall have them in derision' (Ps. 2.4). One is reminded of Kierkegaard's saying that if a philosopher were to argue in my presence that I did not exist, this would be a great impertinence: he would be making a fool of me. If, on the other hand, he were to take his own argument seriously, he would be making a fool of himself.

Empiricism in a Religious Mode

When in the 1920s the logical positivism of the 'Vienna Circle' was driven out of Austria by the rise of Fascism, it found a refuge in Oxford (and elsewhere), where the native British tradition of empiricism was naturally congenial. By 1936 the so-called 'verification principle'[1] had been promulgated and was widely received as an authoritative dogma; it could not, indeed, have been received in any other way, because there is no conceivable means of verifying it.[2] According to the verification principle, it was alleged, all metaphysical, ethical and theological statements must be pronounced neither true nor false, but meaningless. Today, however, the climate has changed somewhat, and no philosopher would describe himself as a logical positivist. The verification principle has been reformulated in new

[1] Cf. A. J. Ayer, *Language, Truth and Logic*, 1st ed., 1936.
[2] The principle declared that only statements (apart from those of pure logic and mathematics) which can be empirically verified or falsified can have meaning; as there is no way of verifying or falsifying this statement empirically, it must therefore be judged meaningless.

ways, and linguistic analysts now often say that the meaning of a word is identical with its use in our language,[1] a statement so comprehensively true that it allows us to hold that words like 'God' can have a meaning after all. But the meaning which some empiricists allow such words to retain is very far from their normative use in biblical and Christian language.

According to religious empiricists of this school of thought, when I say, 'I believe in God', I am not making any meaningful or factual statement about the existence of God; I am merely expressing an attitude, sounding a note of confidence, or affirming my intention to live and act in a certain way. Thus, Professor Braithwaite, relying on the verification principle (old style), tells us that religious assertions, such as that a personal God created the world, are factually meaningless; nevertheless, he says, they have a use, namely, as *moral* assertions: they express the intention of the individual who makes them to act in the sort of way specified in the assertion.[2] The Christian's assertion that God is love, the epitome (in Braithwaite's unhistorical view) of the Christian religion, is merely a declaration of his intention to follow the way of love. The difference between a moral assertion and a religious one is that in the latter there is reference to a 'story' as well as to an intention. In the Christian religion, for example, there is the 'story' of Jesus and all the stories which bear upon his moral significance for the disciple. The story may be part history, part legend, part myth; it does not matter whether the associated story is historical or not, but the story is what differentiates religious belief from a merely moral belief.[3]

[1] Cf. L. Wittgenstein, *Philosophical Investigations*, Oxford, 1958, para. 43.

[2] R. B. Braithwaite, *An Empiricist's View of Religious Belief*, Cambridge, 1955.

[3] Cf. ibid., 32f.: 'A moral belief is an intention to behave in a certain way: a religious belief is an intention to behave in a certain way (a moral belief) together with the entertainment of certain stories associated with the intention in the mind of the believer.'

There are a number of variations of this view amongst empiricist philosophers today,[1] but Braithwaite gives it us in its unadulterated essence. If he is saying that this is what religion means for him, his statements are unexceptionable; but if he is saying that this is the nature of religious belief as such, then his assertions are palpably unfounded. There is no such thing as 'meaning' in general. Meaning is always somebody's meaning—Braithwaite's meaning or my meaning or someone else's. I cannot allow even a Professor of Moral Philosophy to tell me that, when I say that I believe in God, what I really mean is that I intend to behave in accordance with a story which may or may not be true. I certainly do not mean this. For one thing, I am all too conscious that I have little power to behave in the way I intend to behave, story or no story. I mean what I say, namely, that I believe in God, who created me and all mankind and who does not love me or the logical positivists any the less because we entertain inadequate notions about him. Those who believe in the verification principle (in any form) should speak only for themselves, not for those who possess evidence which they will not allow to be brought into court.

The value of the empiricist criticism of the inherited conventional notions about God (*fides historica*[2]) is that it should help Christians to get lingering eighteenth-century deistic ideas about God out of their system. What they are criticizing is not the God of the Bible and the Christian

[1] For example, R. M. Hare's 'blik' view of the nature of faith in *New Essays in Philosophical Theology*, ed. Flew and MacIntyre, London and New York, 1955, 99–103; or Paul van Buren's *Secular Meaning of the Gospel*, New York and London, 1963, where, however, linguistic analysis is combined with existentialist demythologizing and a dash of Bonhoeffer. There are, of course, other empiricist philosophers who do not think that religious belief is only a matter of intentions and stories, e.g. Ian T. Ramsey, *Religious Language*, London, 1957; John Hick, *Faith and Knowledge*, Cornell U.P., 1957; D. D. Evans, *The Logic of Self-Involvement*, London, 1963.
[2] See below, pp. 109–12.

faith, but the conventional Western conception of God, a notional construction built largely upon hearsay and half-understood teaching received in childhood and adolescence. This 'God' is at the intellectual level the integrating principle of a metaphysic called theism, although deism would have been almost as accurate a description. At a less reflective level the 'God' whom the empiricists discuss is the 'God' of Mainstream Religion,[1] which assumes that the word has a meaning plainly understood and generally accepted. The empiricist criticism of the 'God' of hearsay religion will be helpful if it drives Christians to listen more carefully to what the Bible says about God. The God of the Bible and of the Christian faith is not a philosophical speculation, but the living God who makes himself known by his word. The only kind of linguistic analysis which is useful in elucidating the Christian meaning of the word 'God' is that which is undertaken by scholars on the basis of the original languages of the Bible and their related language groups, with all the aid of archaeological, philological, critical and historical expertise which has been developed over the centuries. The English-language linguistic analysis of the empiricists, designed primarily for the clarification of scientific language, is a blunt instrument which resembles a flint axe-head as compared with a precision instrument. The empiricists suffer also from the handicap of working with a non-historical map of language, which prevents any real understanding of the meaning of theological words in their historical context. Theologians who have embarked upon a lively discussion with the empiricists in recent times have often shared too many of their preconceptions to make the dialogue really fruitful. In every age a danger which besets the Christian apologist is that, in his desire to make contact

---

[1] *Mainstream Religion: a Study of the Content of Religious Broadcasting during June, 1963*, compiled by the William Temple College, Rugby, published in 1965.

with those occupying entrenched positions beyond no-man's-land, he will go too far in the direction of his opponents' categories and be unable to regain his proper ground. This is what happened to the great Bishop Butler in the eighteenth century, and the consequence is that his defence of Christian truth against deism hardly stood the test of time. Both Butler and his opponents lacked an understanding of history and of its importance for language study.

The Christian Significance of Atheism

We are often told nowadays that we live in an atheistic age. Before we start repeating this shibboleth, we had better examine it more closely. It is true that in this enlightened television age one has to be a bishop before one can startle folk by declaring oneself an atheist. But if we submit the shibboleth to the test of the verification principle, that the meaning of a statement is identical with the method of its verification, we soon notice that it is meaningless. It cannot be empirically verified. There are millions of Roman Catholics, Protestants, Mohammedans, Jews and others who believe in God; and even in Russia, where all the resources of the State have been employed for nearly half a century on the inculcation of atheism, there are still some thirty-three million Orthodox Christians. We must take the statement to mean a declaration on the part of those who make it that they intend to live as if there were no God, whatever may be the 'stories' they associate with their intention (e.g. Bertrand Russell's 'vast death of the solar system' or van Buren's gospel story as re-edited by Bultmann).[1] But we should look more deeply than this, if only because during the last thirty years the verification principle has

[1] Bonhoeffer's enigmatic remarks about 'living in the world as if there were no God' can hardly be taken to support an atheistic view, since he tells us that *God* makes us know that we must live as men who can get along without him (*Letters and Papers from Prison*, 163f.).

60

itself already 'died the death of a thousand qualifications'.

Atheism, as we understand the word today, is a modern phenomenon, intelligible only in a Christian civilization. The Greek word 'atheist' did not mean one who denied the existence of God or the supernatural, but rather one who refused to venerate the imperial or civic deities, and was therefore suspected of disloyalty to the political order or indeed of worse crimes. Thus, Socrates was condemned to death on a charge of atheism, but he was not an atheist in the modern sense. Similarly the Jews were accounted atheists, because they would not worship at Caesar's shrine or take part in the games in honour of the pagan gods. When the Christian martyr Polycarp was tried at Smyrna in AD 155, the proconsul urged him to cry, 'Away with the atheists', meaning that Polycarp should affirm his loyalty to Caesar and the State divinities; Polycarp complied and cried 'Away with the atheists', but he meant those who worshipped the false gods of politics and luck, who had usurped the honour of the one true God of all the earth. And so Polycarp was burnt on a charge of 'pulling down our gods' by those whom he called atheists.[1] At an earlier date the author of the Epistle to the Ephesians (St Paul or someone writing in his name) referred to the Christians recently converted from paganism as having formerly had no hope and being atheists in the world (Eph. 2.12); he meant that, when they knew only the pagan gods, they were without hope and therefore without divine aid in the world, with all its anxieties and afflictions. He does not mean that they were atheists in the modern sense, for they had worshipped the well-known deities of the contemporary 'mainstream religion'.[2]

---

[1] The Martyrdom of Polycarp, J. B. Lightfoot, *Apostolic Fathers*, 1898, 206f.
[2] Eph. 2.12 is the only place in which the word 'atheist' occurs in the Bible; the Greek word here is *atheoi*, 'godless'.

Atheism, as we speak of it today, can be understood only against a Christian (or at least a biblical) background. It would, for example, be pointless to use the word in the context of Buddhism, in which the idea of a creating and ruling deity is entirely absent. Atheism can define itself only by reference to God, conceived or misconceived in biblical terms. In the post-renaissance era it has arisen chiefly as a revolt against the identification of Christianity with some outmoded system of thought or social order which is passionately felt to impede the progress of mankind in the direction of those very ideals which the Christian world view has itself made possible. It is a sobering thought for Christians that all the major atheistic movements of modern times, from the rationalism of the Enlightenment to the persecuting zeal of Marxist-Leninist materialism, are the bitter fruit of the Church's compromise with effete and repressive social systems or of her reluctance to embrace new ways of thought. In individual cases, too, we may notice how often a reasonable and humane person has become an atheist by way of reaction from the stern conventionalism or the saccharine sentimentality or the intellectual laziness of well-meaning parents or teachers. Wherever there is a passionate atheist, there is a failure of Christian charity or courage somewhere in the background. It would be impossible to speak of an atheistic age if a Christian civilization were not its background, for except in terms of revulsion from Christian teaching and practice the word 'atheism' has no meaning. It is for this reason that Christians should take the phenomenon of atheism very seriously. To fulminate against atheism, to revile it, or to ignore it, even to be content with arguing against it, is to miss the divinely directed challenge of atheism to a Church that is unable to see the beam in its own eye. Atheism in the modern world is an occasion of penitence for the Church.

But Christians have no need to fear atheism, for atheism,

like the idols of pagan religion, has no independent existence; it could not exist save as an instrument of God's merciful correction of the sins of Christians. In the western world in the recent past intellectual laziness has been one of the most serious of those sins; charges of dishonesty, which are sometimes brought against Christians, are probably exaggerated. Christians must not expect to escape without travail from the consequences of their derelictions; we must heed the warning that the full impact of modern atheism still lies ahead of us.[1] They must welcome the passionate atheist, not shun or fear him. His zeal for truth or for social righteousness is his personal obedience to the promptings within him of the God he does not know. In so far as he is in earnest about truth and justice, he is to be counted as one who denies Christ for Christ's sake. It is true that he may cause some of Christ's little ones to stumble, but if he is judged by the intention and not by the result, no millstone shall be hung around his neck: Christ's word was spoken not to the honest doubter but to the faithless disciple. Christ's parable of the two sons, the one who said he would go and did not, and the other who said he would not go but did, is relevant here (Matt. 21.28-31). The passionate atheist is a witness to the truth, not only by reason of his reforming zeal, but also because of his very words. He cannot promulgate his atheism without calling attention to the existence of God, and so he is a witness in spite of himself; he is so much more useful than the discreetly silent Christian, because he is always reminding people of the God whom they so easily forget.

We have spoken of the 'passionate' atheist rather than the 'good' atheist, because goodness, whether of atheists or Christians, is always the fruit of the divine grace and can be judged only by him to whom all hearts are open and all

[1] G. Ebeling, *Word and Faith*, Eng. trans., London and Philadelphia, 1963, 342.

desires known. But there is another kind of atheist, who by contrast with the passionate atheist might be called the practical atheist, and he is the sort of atheist who should be feared. We should fear him because he may be our own self. There is no danger that anyone will ever disprove God, but there is every danger that tomorrow you and I will forget him. For God is the active God, who challenges us and disturbs us. He demands our worship and obedience in every detail of our life. His absolute holiness reproves our selfishness and bids us care for others. It is so much easier to forget him and just live our own life, hoping that he will leave us alone in the same tolerant fashion that we leave him alone, so that we can concentrate on ourselves, our interests, pleasures, profession, amusements, friends and family, and generally enjoy ourselves in our own way. Then, when we have forgotten about him for a long time, and when we are perhaps feeling a little guilty about our neglect of him, how comforting it is to be persuaded that he does not 'really' exist. The verification principle, or an argument from psychology or cosmology, comes along as a kind of anti-gospel, an anti-saviour which bears away our sins and gives us the anti-satisfaction of a clear and adult anti-conscience. This is the kind of atheist whom we should fear, the atheist who lives in our own heart.

SUGGESTIONS FOR FURTHER READING

John Baillie, *Invitation to Pilgrimage*, Oxford, 1942.

John Hick (ed.), *Faith and the Philosophers*, London and New York, 1964.

Gerhard Ebeling, *Word and Faith*, Eng. trans., London and Philadelphia, 1963, 333–62.

Helmut Gollwitzer, *The Existence of God*, Eng. trans., London and Philadelphia, 1965.

4

COSMOLOGY AND LANGUAGE

PROFESSOR Helmut Gollwitzer of the Free University of Berlin contributed to *Der Spiegel* in June 1964, a judicious review of the German edition of Bishop J. A. T. Robinson's *Honest to God*.[1] He referred to the astonishing sensation created by an accident: the editor of *The Observer*, finding a commissioned article unsuitable, printed instead an article summarizing the Bishop's book, supplying it liberally with headlines (which the Bishop did not write) such as 'Our Image of God Must Go'.[2] Dr Gollwitzer points to the unavoidable conclusion that our whole system of religious education must have failed dismally, if the readers of the 'quality' Sunday papers should have been thus surprised when a bishop made 'public' the views of theologians which had in fact been commonplace for half a century, and which had been available for all to read in hundreds of books and periodicals in every bookshop and library in the land. The British educated public would appear to be almost as ignorant of contemporary theological thinking as the citizens of Soviet Russia. One is reminded of an incident recorded in another book of Dr Gollwitzer's. There he describes how, as a prisoner of war in Russia, he was interrogated by some Red Army officers who had discovered that he possessed a doctor's degree of a German university.

[1] London, 1963. Gollwitzer's review is printed as an appendix to his book *The Existence of God*, Eng. trans., London and Philadelphia, 1965, 247–51.
[2] The London *Observer*, Sunday, 17 March 1963.

' "What sort of a doctor?" they ask. Theology. What was that? I try to explain to them. They come down to earth: that is not a science—and they eagerly inform me that science and religion are diametrically opposed to each other. That we can study theology at a university is for them proof of the incomprehensible backwardness of the West.'[1]

The Biblical World View and Modern Scientific Cosmology

Everyone who has ever tried to answer a child's questions about where God is knows just how exhaustingly impossible the attempt can be. The difficulty is that the child has no concept of immaterial reality: for him the 'real' is what has tangible existence in space and time. Even angels and fairies, if they are real to him at all, must have bodies of some kind. Very often in adolescence the child dismisses religious truth altogether, because he has not learnt the proper use of language which describes spiritual realities under pictorial forms drawn from the physical world. Our religious education has so often failed, because in a climate of opinion which regards scientific language as the only meaningful language, it has failed to get across the true character of religious language as analogical. A degree of spiritual maturity is necessary before one can speak the language of religion. Adolescents are naturally literalistically minded and in their logic a thing is either literally true or it is not true in any sense. Either God created the world in six days or the world was not created by God at all; either Jesus ascended in bodily form through the clouds to a physical heaven above the earth, or St Luke's story in Acts has no meaning of any kind. Many middle-aged and elderly people have failed to grow beyond this immature stage, and their arrested development is even taken by some religious

[1] *Unwilling Journey*, London and Philadelphia, 1953, Eng. trans. of *Und führen, wohin du nicht willst*, Munich, 1951.

spokesmen today to be a sign that men have 'come of age'. Anyone who has tried to explain to such adults the true meaning of 'he ascended into heaven' knows that the difficulty of answering the questions of children is as a mole-hill in comparison with that of removing a lifetime's mis-understanding of the deeper issues of human experience.

We should, however, be careful to notice what the difficulty is. It does not concern questions of physics and cosmology. Natural science can tell us nothing about the ultimate nature of reality, whether it is material and purposeless or spiritual and having a goal. It is unlikely that such questions can ever be answered by science. As Sir Cyril Hinshel-wood said in his presidential address to the British Association at Cambridge,[1] at all the boundaries of science we come up against what are probably the inherent limitations of human understanding. At the edge of biology we meet the chasm between what science describes and what the mind experiences. In the physical sciences, too, we encounter insoluble contradictions if we try to contemplate the limits of space or the beginning of time. But at least, without crossing the frontiers which Sir Cyril describes, we can perceive that it is easier to believe that mind rather than matter is the index of reality, now that physicists themselves suppose an elaborate mathematical formula to be a better 'model' of the physical world than the old pre-quantum model of an infinite number of billiard balls rattling about in a box called space, a box which had no sides or top or bottom. Science does not answer our questions 'why'. Why should numerical and geometrical laws govern the transient entities of the sub-atomic world? Or, to pose the fundamental ontological question of Heidegger, why should being *be* at all—why should there not simply be Nothing? We can turn away from such a question and say (with the positivists) that, because science cannot answer it, it is therefore

[1] 1 September 1965.

meaningless; but that is itself an answer, just as scientifically undemonstrable as any other. Yet the question presses relentlessly upon us, and despite the positivists, we are compelled to face it in the moment of coming face to face with ourselves. Why should I *be*? Why should not I not be? The mere fact that we can pose the question about our being would seem to challenge us to seek for a purpose in our *being*. In other words, our very existence faces us with an ethical and religious decision about ourselves. The determining factor in leading men to answer the ontological question, whether positively or negatively, has always been their personal response to the challenge of their own existence. In one of his earlier books Professor John Baillie wrote: 'What was it, ultimately, that put Leucippus, Epicurus, Hobbes, d'Holbach and Mr (Bertrand) Russell into one camp and Socrates, Plato, Descartes, Berkeley and T. H. Green into the other? We submit that nothing had more to do with it than the initial weight they were willing to give to our ethico-religious insights.'[1]

The real difficulty, therefore, about answering such questions as 'Where is God?' is not created by modern scientific cosmology at all. The problem is one of language, how to find a means of communicating with one another in the sphere of personal and ethical and religious ideas and values. This is a sphere beyond the possibility of measurement and therefore outside the scope of science. Thoroughgoing positivists would say that it is therefore entirely unreal and illusory, but such a view contradicts the universal moral experience of the human race. There is no barometer which can measure the pressure of a man's conscience; no thermometer can record the intensity of his aesthetic enjoyment; levels of virtue cannot be plotted on a graph; pride and selfishness, courage and sympathy cannot be weighed or calibrated. Are moral or aesthetic or spiritual values there-

[1] *The Interpretation of Religion*, Edinburgh, 1929, 39.

fore unreal? Dr Baillie is right: the camp in which a man finds himself will in the last resort be determined by the initial weight he is willing to give to moral and religious insights; it is a matter of personal decision. Is the terrifying silence of infinite space[1] the last word on the subject of the mystery around us, or is the mind of a man who can calculate that the Andromeda nebula is 750,000 light-years away a more likely clue to the secret of the universe? Should the immensity of space and time oppress us, if (as the philosopher Immanuel Kant suggested some two hundred years ago) they are not things in themselves but only the forms of our perception? Our difficulty in thinking about ultimate questions does not arise from the scientific world view itself but from the fact that we have not learned to speak a language which deals with realities beyond the vocabulary of science. The Bible develops its own language by which it can speak of things which are beyond the possibility of treatment by means of the scientific method; its language is therefore compatible with any stage of scientific development, because, though it inevitably uses the thought-forms of its day, it is not a book about cosmology and we do not go to it for answers to scientific questions. In order to accept the teaching of the Bible about God and human destiny we do not have first to accomplish the impossible task of transforming ourselves back into men of the first century AD or to imagine that Aristotle and Ptolemy are nearer to the truth than Darwin and Einstein.

How far should we Demythologize?

Where is God? If we expect a literal answer to this question, we are as foolish as those who thought that Laplace's telescope should have located him, or that the Russian cosmonauts had disproved his existence because they had

[1] Pascal, *Pensées*, iii. 206.

traversed the heavens and not found him there. The Bible knows better than this. Most modern people confuse the late mediaeval picture of the three-story universe, based on the Ptolemaic astronomy, with the biblical view itself. Bultmann has done an immense disservice by putting it about that the New Testament writers believed literally in a three-story universe with heaven 'up there' and hell beneath our feet. The truth is that, like the Old Testament writers, they did not locate God in any particular place at all. For the biblical writers God is everywhere and he is nowhere. He is everywhere: 'If I ascend up into heaven, thou art there; if I make my bed in Sheol (hell), behold, thou art there. If I take the wings of the morning and dwell in the uttermost parts of the sea, even there shall thy hand lead me.' The Psalmist knows that God is everywhere at the same time throughout the universe and that it is impossible to flee from his presence (Ps. 139.7-12). This means that God is in no particular *place*; he is no more in heaven than he is on the earth: 'Behold, the heaven of heavens cannot contain thee,' cries King Solomon, 'how much less this house that I have built' (I Kings 8.27). God is not *outside* the universe, but neither is he *inside* it as one of its parts; he made the universe, including the heavens, which along with the earth shall one day pass away like smoke (Isa. 51.6); God is contrasted with the heavens as well as with the earth as the permanent is contrasted with the ephemeral (Ps. 102.25-7; cf. Heb. 1.10-2). This is a poetical way of saying that God is not in space and time at all, at least not in the sense that we are. God was God before the foundation of the world, and he will still be God after it has passed away.

When the Bible connects God with a particular place, when it says that he dwells among Israel or that he has set his name in Jerusalem, this does not mean that he is 'there' any more than in Babylon or China, but that he was *known* to be near at certain moments in the history of Israel or

Cosmology and Language

Jerusalem. The geographical references to such places as Sinai or Mount Zion are really historical references; all the geography of the Bible is in a profound sense *historical geography*.[1] The biblical writers had no cosmology of their own; they borrowed their 'scientific world view' (for such it was in their day) from their contemporaries, the Babylonians or (later) the Greeks. It is impossible to construct a biblical cosmology, for many stages of cosmological development are represented in the various parts of the Bible; and, since what they were talking about was neither science in general nor cosmology in particular, the truth of what they said is not bound up with the validity of any particular scientific world view. They were speaking about a reality which concerns us more intimately than the physical universe can ever do, even though the world seems so much with us. They were speaking about God, and what they have to say is equally relevant to men who believed that the earth floats on water and is covered by an inverted pudding-basin (the firmament in which the stars are set) or to men living in the space age who listen to Third Programme talks on astrophysics. There is no such thing as a biblical cosmology; as Professor Boman of Oslo has said, 'What we call the cosmological ideas of the Bible are virtually the cosmological ideas of the Middle Ages; they are neither Hebrew nor Greek, but a naïve mixture of both.'[2]

There is no danger of conflict between the Bible and modern cosmological science. But there is every likelihood of a clash between the biblical language and modern sophistication. One kind of contemporary sophistication is that which assumes that imaginative language, striving to express in pictures what scientific prose cannot utter, is meaningless because it is not literally true and is not trans-

[1] Cf. Thorleif Boman, *Hebrew Thought Compared with Greek*, Eng. trans., London and Philadelphia, 1960, 182f., where relevant references will conveniently be found.
[2] Op. cit., 183.

71

latable into scientific phraseology. Yet most of us have happily not reached the stage of sophistication which is unable to appreciate poetic truth. When the biblical writer makes Jehovah say, 'The heaven is my throne and the earth is my footstool' (Isa. 66.1; cf. Matt. 5.34f.), he does not mean that God sits in heaven with his feet on the earth,[1] but is expressing the relationship between the realm where God's will is perfectly fulfilled and the earthly kingdoms which, though they may not acknowledge it, are nevertheless subject to his authority (cf. Matt. 6.10, the Lord's Prayer). When the biblical writers wish to express the infinite qualitative distinction between God and man, they say, 'God is in heaven and thou art upon earth' (Eccles. 5.2), with no more thought of a spatial relation in their mind than when they portray man's overweening pride as an exalting of himself to heaven (Isa. 14.13f.; Ezek. 28.2; Matt. 11.23: 'And thou, Capernaum, shalt thou be exalted into heaven? thou shalt go down into Hades'). In the Bible heaven and hell are not *places*, geographically identifiable; they are pictorial representations of nearness to God through obedience to his will or of distance from God occasioned by rebellion against it.

How far should we demythologize? For the most part, not at all, because the biblical writers have done the job for us already. It is we who have forgotten the art of poetic communication; and so we create a problem by our sophisticated literal-mindedness. It is we, not the biblical writers, who take the stories of the Bible literally and therefore find it necessary to demythologize them. For example, there is little reason to suppose that those who first told the story of the Tower of Babel (Gen. 11.1-9) thought that it was a literally true story. Even the most primitive of men (and the J writer of Genesis certainly is not that!) must have noticed that if one climbed the highest mountain or the loftiest

[1] Boman, ibid.

zikkurat (terraced tower) in Babylon (= Babel), one is just as far away from the sky as one had been on the level plain. The story is a parable concerning the futility of man's attempt to build civilization on a foundation other than the divine law of justice and to impose unity on subject races by military and economic power—which is, of course, just what Babylon was ruthlessly attempting all through her years of imperial grandeur. The result is not unity, but scattering and confusion, a babel confusion of the language of humanity, so that nation can no longer speak with nation or people unto people. The story contains a truth far deeper than any mere pre-scientific guess-work at how the various tribes came to speak different tongues.[1]

In the New Testament, too, stories with profound symbolical significance are told in a matter-of-fact way which misleads the literalistic Western mind. St Luke's story of the Ascension is a good example: we are simply told that the Risen Jesus was 'taken up' into heaven and that a cloud received him out of the sight of the disciples (Acts 1.9). We have little idea what in fact were St Luke's cosmological notions, but we may be sure that he was not thinking about cosmology at all: he is not telling us about the ascent of a physical body to a place above the sky. Heaven is not a *place* for the biblical writers, and there is no need to suppose that St Luke is an exception to the rule. It was natural for the New Testament writers to use a metaphor drawn from an oriental court, where the Grand Vizier sat at the right hand of the King (cf. Eph. 1.20; Col. 3.1; cp. Acts 7.56), but it would be precarious to suppose that they intended anything more than a metaphor. The marriage of Hebraic thought and Greek science had as yet not taken place and we must not read back later ideas into the apostolic age. The cloud in St Luke's story is a well-known symbol of the

[1] For the fuller exegesis of Gen. 11.1–9 see Alan Richardson, *Genesis I–XI*, Torch Commentaries, London, 1953.

73

mystery of the divine presence in both the Old and the New Testaments, and St Luke knew that his readers would understand this; he was not in the least interested in the meteorological phenomena at the time, but was using traditional symbols to describe a truth which he well knew was beyond the power of words to convey except in pictures and images. If we want to understand the Bible, we must try to understand it as its earliest readers would have done. They would have understood St Luke's Ascension story to mean just what Christians have always held the doctrine of Christ's Ascension to imply: that this Jesus, with whom the apostles had companied in Galilee and Judea, was in a unique sense the eternal revelation of God, whose Spirit was now no longer confined within an historical person in a particular corner of the world, but was at one with the universal God of all the earth and was yet present to men everywhere across all space and all time. St Luke, the historian of the expansion of the apostolic Church, knew from his own experience of the Christian mission that Jesus was not dead but was the present Lord of the whole great world movement which had begun from Jerusalem. The missionaries did not take Christ to India: they found him there.'[1] Do we really need to demythologize St Luke's story of the Ascension? We would not need to do so, if we had not first made the mistake of regarding it as a piece of descriptive cosmology.

That which cannot be Demythologized

It is impossible to demythologize things which are not

[1] Cf. *Aikya*, the magazine of the Student Christian Movement of India, Vol. II, No. 4, April 1965, article by R. W. Rentoul, 'The Indian Church and the Ascension': 'In order to show India that Christ is universal we must show also that he is Indian. We should not be afraid of taking over and absorbing the culture of India as it is, as already belonging to Christ. For the Ascension meant that Christ belonged to each country even as he belonged to all. . . .'

myths. The great Christian doctrines, such as that of the Ascension of Christ, are not myths, even though in their New Testament form they are often stated in the language of poetry rather than in dogmatic constructions such as theologians subsequently used to explain their meaning in more sophisticated times. It is true that certain episodes in the Gospels would be described by us in twentieth-century ways and not in terms of the 'scientific' views of the first century AD. For instance, we would not describe insanity or deafness or a storm at sea in terms of demon possession; but, however we would describe such phenomena, the facts about mental and physical illness or about natural phenomena remain what they were in the days of the apostles, who still confront us with their testimony that Jesus was lord over them. The pictures which we might use to convey the truth concerning the inevitability of divine judgment or of the goal of history would doubtless not be embellished with first-century Jewish ideas about angels, furnaces, cosmic convulsions and divine law-courts, but must we be so sophisticated and unimaginative as to be unable to discern the moral and religious truths which are latent in them? We can, if we wish, call the process of interpreting the ancient symbols 'demythologizing', but the danger of so doing is that we shall fall into Bultmann's error of assuming that the New Testament writers took their own picture language literally and we may thus be tempted to substitute some modern existentialist notions for the plain and true meaning of the Gospels. If we start from the notion that the Gospel writers were rather unintelligent men, who mistook Gnostic or apocalyptic nonsense for literal truth and lived in a dream world of pre-scientific fancy, we shall end up, as Bultmann does, by demythologizing the Gospel history out of existence.

What cannot be demythologized is historical fact. It is true, of course, that what we call the 'facts' of history are only interpretations of evidence. But history (as an art and as a science) is concerned with nothing else than the interpretation of evidence and it is based upon the assumption that one interpretation of the evidence can be shown to be more credible than another. One fact—that is, a judgment of evidence upon which almost all historians have agreed—is that the Church in which and for which the Gospels were written came into existence as a result of the life and work of Jesus of Nazareth, who was put to death under Pontius Pilatus, the Roman procurator of Judea from AD 26 to 36. It would seem surprising that a mission which had ended in failure on the gallows should have given birth to a movement that has shaped a world-wide civilization, which, though now largely secularized, cannot deny its Christian origin. In point of fact, every book in the New Testament points to the conclusion that it was upon the conviction that Jesus was alive after his crucifixion that this great world enterprise was founded. Bultmann and some of his followers have done their best to 'demythologize' the resurrection of Jesus, which they regard as being not an historical event but only a mythological way of presenting the deeply felt significance of his death. But the resurrection of Jesus remains stubbornly resistant to the process of demythologizing; it thrusts itself back into history as the only credible historical explanation of the coming into existence of the Church, if we have regard to the circumstances in which Jesus died. The resurrection of Christ must be accounted an historical fact, that is, the most credible interpretation of the available evidence, and therefore one of the things which cannot be demythologized.[1] When it is said that Christianity is an historical religion, what is meant is that it is founded upon and was called into existence by the actual

[1] A full discussion of the historical character of Christ's resurrection will be found in Alan Richardson, *History Sacred and Profane*, London and Philadelphia, 1964, 182–212.

occurrence of certain definite historical events. The historical evidence, as it has come down to us, points to the *fact* that faith in Jesus did not create the belief in his resurrection (cf. Luke 24.20f.), but that the resurrection of Jesus created faith in Jesus and therefore also the Church which arose to bear witness to his resurrection.

Words and the Word

Animals, it has been wisely said, do not speak because they have nothing to say. Men, too, are silent about those matters on which they have nothing to say. They develop a language only when they have something to communicate. First-century men did not develop the language of modern science, because they had nothing to say from our modern scientific point of view. Many twentieth-century men do not speak the language of religion because they have no experience or conviction to speak about. Perhaps they have been too preoccupied in mastering a specialized language, such as that of science or of business; in addition, they have found that it takes all their time to acquire the language of 'admass', that is, the language which 'everyone' speaks and which one simply must keep up with, if one is to be considered 'with it' or 'switched on' (or whatever the current admass jargon decrees the fashionable term). For such people the language of the Bible, of religion, of liturgical worship and probably also of morals, in the sense of deeper personal relationships, is a dead language; they can understand most of the words, but they cannot speak the language, because the language does not speak to them. Religious language does not communicate with anything in their unauthentic lives, because nothing ultimate, nothing existential, nothing real is ever allowed to break through the protecting walls of conventional nonentity. No new translations of the Bible, no contemporary liturgical forms, no demythologized or 'non-religious' presentations of man's basic concern, will enable secularized and dehumanized people to speak a language which they have felt no need to speak.

The most important thing about man is his language; this is a truth which we might have learned from the Bible, but since it has recently been most strongly emphasized by a modern philosopher, we shall give special attention in our next chapter to Martin Heidegger. There is a profound sense in which a man's humanity is defined by his language. We all know what is meant when we hear someone say, 'So-and-so speaks my language'; it is implied that there is a community of understanding, a common point of view, between the persons concerned; they understand each other. This community of understanding is what is so often lacking between peoples and groups. They do not see things from the other's point of view; they do not speak one another's language; they understand only the language of their own trade or class or interest, their own race or culture. Despite a common technological *lingua franca*, which every year more and more people of many different nationalities throughout the world are learning to speak, they do not speak a common language of humanity. Scientific-technological language cannot itself become the wholly adequate common language of humanity; it is very important, and we all need to learn it, because, rightly used, it can form the substructure of the great scientifically based civilization of the future. But if not supplemented by the language of the Spirit, it can build only a Babel-tower whose top will never reach heaven and whose outcome will be only a scattering of the nations and a confusion of language. It has no power to restrain the demonic voices of nationalism and of ideologies based upon sectional interests and not upon the needs and consciences of mankind as a whole. The cloven tongue of the serpent will always be at hand to beguile men with the flattering promise, 'Ye shall be as gods, making your own good and evil' (Gen. 3.5), and men in their pride will emulate Babylon in seeking to create a false unity of humanity by military and economic power, using all the resources of science and technology, even the conquest of space itself, to make for themselves a 'name' (Gen. 11.4) which will usurp the place of the name of God, to which alone worship and honour are due. St Luke, in his parabolic story of the gift of the Spirit at Pentecost, describes in poetic, biblical imagery how the lost unity of the human race is recreated by the power of the Holy Spirit of God (Acts 2.5-11). Significantly his story is one which deals profoundly with the theme of language, in which is located both the origin and the final resolution of the human predicament. St Luke's story is the story of Babel in reverse. Men who formerly could not speak to one another in a common tongue, because they had no common interest or mutual concern, are recreated by the gift of the Holy Spirit into one family, no longer estranged by diversities of nationality, religion, culture or language. This was the actual experience of the earliest Christian Church, in which 'men from every nation under heaven' heard, each in his own tongue, the proclamation of the wonderful works of God. St Luke in his parable is using the familiar phenomenon of 'speaking with tongues' (*glossolalia*), which seems to have characterized the meetings of the earliest Christian communities (and indeed it has appeared at many later times); and by it he conveys a truth far deeper than the mere literalistic description of the scene, the awareness that the proper unity of mankind is based upon a divinely given common language which God intends all men to speak.

These things, like all the truths touching the human spirit or the deeper levels of our humanity, are far beyond the power of ordinary everyday words to describe. Perhaps therefore it would be well to call to our aid an articulation of

79

them by a modern poet, who in a few lines has expressed much more adequately those truths about language and the unity of mankind which we have been attempting to enunciate in this chapter:

> When the tower of Babel fell
> All accord by words was lost
> Till the Holy Ghost came down
> Bringing hope at Pentecost.
>
> Cloven tongues twice spoke to man,
> First a serpent at the fall,
> Then as flames which lit and ran
> Till men of one speech could speak to all.
>
> Let the holy Spirit come,
> Come with fire of Pentecost,
> Forge again with tongues of flame
> The common tongue we had and lost.[1]

SUGGESTIONS FOR FURTHER READING

Edwyn Bevan, *Symbolism and Belief*, London, 1938; Fontana edition, 1962.

Austin Farrer, *The Glass of Vision*, London, 1948.

Alan Richardson, *Preface to Bible Study*, London and Philadelphia, 1943.

Alan Richardson, *Genesis I–XI* (Torch Commentary), London, 1953.

Ian T. Ramsey, *Christian Discourse: Some Logical Explorations*, Oxford and New York, 1965.

[1] Audrey Beecham, set to music by Ivor Keys as an anthem for Whit Sunday, 'Prayer for Pentecostal Fire', Oxford Univ. Press (A169), 1961.

5

THE NEW HERMENEUTICS

MODERN thought since the eighteenth century has developed out of the on-going dialogue between philosophy and theology. Today this dialogue continues with unabated vigour on the European continent and in America. As a result of it new formulations and perspectives are arising. For the last forty years a debate has been conducted by theologians in dialogue with Martin Heidegger (born 1889) and his followers. It began during the years in which Rudolf Bultmann's long tenure of the Professorship of New Testament at Marburg coincided with the short period in which Heidegger was Professor of Philosophy there (1923-28) and Tillich was his colleague. Bultmann developed his existentialist theology under the influence of Heidegger, while Tillich (we are told) learned from Heidegger that 'being' is the most appropriate way of speaking about God, because it is the only non-symbolic way of referring to him. Heidegger, though in his youth a Jesuit seminarian at Freiburg, does not speak about God at all, and refuses to identify 'being' with God. It would seem that, like Tillich, he regards his philosophy as having transcended both theism and atheism, since it elucidates the disclosure of being, beyond which there is nothing that we can know or need to know.

The Earlier Heidegger

In 1927 Heidegger's *Sein und Zeit*[1] was published. It came

[1] Eng. trans. by John Macquarrie and Edward Robinson, *Being and*

to be widely regarded as the New Testament of existentialism, fulfilling the established Old Testament canon, which was, of course, identified with the writings of Sören Kierkegaard in the previous century. But whereas Kierkegaard had grounded man's existence in God, Heidegger now proclaimed that he had 'overcome' the traditional metaphysical quest for a transcendent ground of man's being by his discovery that man was grounded in nothing beyond himself. This 'nothing' is very important for Heidegger. Man is *Dasein*, that is, he is simply 'there', poised over nothing, 'thrown' into the world and there abandoned for death. The existentialist analysis proceeds to a phenomenological description of *Dasein*, that is, of man's being-in-the-world. His life is characterized by dread, the unspecific fear of nothing-in-particular: note again the significance of 'nothing', which is yet something to be afraid of. The unauthentic man is the man who dares not face reality (which is, in a sense, 'nothing'). He will not face the fact that one day he will die; he hides himself in the crowd, thinks what everyone else thinks, admires what everyone else admires, not daring to be himself. His talking is not real speaking but is merely idle chatter or gossip, the repetition of everyone else's clichés, the retailing of second-hand opinions, disguised as 'the latest' ideas or fashions, so that he may enjoy the comforting illusion that he is abreast of the times and therefore someone in the know and to be reckoned with. In contrast with unauthentic men ('*das man*') the truly authentic man is the one who has faced the fact that he is poised over the metaphysical nothing and that one day he will die, and who therefore has the possibility of freedom to speak his own words and to live his own life, unsupported by illusions of self-importance, status and being up-to-date.

Time, London and New York, 1962, from the eighth German edition of 1957.

It is hardly surprising that the view articulated in *Being and Time* should have been generally regarded as both existentialist and atheistic, or that Jean-Paul Sartre's *L'Existentialisme est un Humanisme*[1] (1946) should have been deemed its natural child. Sartre is a passionate atheist and his heroic existentialism is a splendid attempt to create meaning in defiance of the meaningless universe which he contemplates. Heidegger, however, promptly disowned his 'French counterpart', rejecting Sartre's theory that existence (*existentia*) precedes essence (*essentia*) as the kind of metaphysics which he himself had transcended and denying that he was himself an existentialist.[2] *Being and Time*, Heidegger[2] pointed out, was an unfinished work; it was only preparing the way for his completed philosophy, which was concerned not with nothing but with being. (It is usual in English to write being without a capital in order to make it clear that Heidegger's being is not the God of theology, as Heidegger himself insists.)

Existentialist or not, it is difficult to regard the standpoint of *Being and Time* as anything other than atheistic. Atheistic, that is to say, in the sense defined above, namely, as owing the truth which it possesses to Christian insights and inconceivable except as a reaction from Christian belief in God. Heidegger's profound and searching account of man's position in the world is a secularized version of the negative part of the New Testament doctrine of man, especially St Paul's; it is a 'phenomenological' description of modern secularized man as 'having no hope and without God in the world' (Eph. 2.11). This 'atheistic' man, however, is of the practical, not the passionate, kind, the man who is blind to the evidences of God's gracious reality all around him, the

[1] Eng. trans. by B. Frechtman, *Existentialism*, New York, Philosophical Library, 1947. Cf. also Sartre's *Being and Nothingness*, 1943.
[2] Heidegger's comment of 1947 was republished as *Über den Humanismus*, Frankfurt/Main, 1949.

evidences which, in fact, Heidegger studiously ignores. The New Testament knows not only of men who are carelessly ignorant of God but also of men who dimly worship God the Unknown (Acts 17.23), men who were created 'that they should seek after God, if haply they might feel after him and find him' (17.27). It knows of Gentiles whose God-given conscience leads them to do by nature the things of God's law (Rom. 2.14), and it knows also of the God who is not far from them (Acts 17.27). Germanic 'neo-orthodoxy'— Barth, Brunner, Bonhoeffer and Bultmann—explained away these New Testament insights in its depreciation of 'religion' as something which the revelation in Christ had abolished, not fulfilled. Heidegger's 'existential analysis' of atheistic (modern) man is in harmony with the neo-orthodox estimate of religious man, and that is why Bultmann could make it the 'pre-understanding' of his existentialist theology. (It also explains why Bultmann dislikes the 'turn' in Heidegger's thinking since 1927.) 'Anthropology' (in the sense of the doctrine of human nature) is a very important part of theology, because God cannot be known in himself but only in his relation to man. The error of the Barthian theology (and of all the neo-orthodox theology) arises from its false start from the modern and unbiblical notion of atheistic man, the man who mistakenly imagines himself to be ignorant of God, autonomous ('come of age'), self-reliant, creating his own good and evil.[1] This is also the error of the Heideggerian existentialist analysis of *Dasein* in *Being and Time*. That analysis is at once illuminating and disturbing, profoundly moving and very sad. Its wide appeal proves that it speaks to the condition of many European intellectuals in an age which has lost its traditional bearings. It is sad, however, because it is so one-sided in its deliberate ignoring of all the radiance, the moral awareness, the

[1] Cf. the Swedish theologian Gustaf Wingren, *Theology in Conflict*, Edinburgh and Philadelphia, 1958, 23–44.

glimpses of holiness, the intimations of succour, which would have to be noted by a more objective analysis. Human life contains something more than the sense of being projected not by our own will into the universe and there abandoned for death; it contains also intimations of immortality, however these may be interpreted, as is evidenced by the religions of the world. Such intimations would not, of course, in themselves provide a gospel, an assurance of final victory; but the Christian has grounds for hoping that being abandoned for death is not man's ultimate fate. He knows something of the experience of having been 'projected' (not by his own will, as the sacrament of infant baptism reminds us) into the Church, the redeemed community of Christ, in which death has lost its sting.

The Later Heidegger

It seems undeniable that, since the publication of the (still uncompleted) *Being and Time* in 1927, there has occurred a change in the direction of Heidegger's thinking. Heidegger himself speaks of a 'turn' in his thought, but insists that it does not involve a radical break with *Being and Time*[1]. Others have likened it to a religious conversion (*Umkehr* rather than *Kehre*). Heidegger and his followers regard his thinking as having accomplished a revolution in philosophy in much the same way as the English linguistic philosophers regard *their* revolution;[2] nevertheless the two revolutions have nothing in common except the conceit of each that it has abolished metaphysics. 'Metaphysics' is often nowadays

[1] For a full documentation of this and similar points see *The Later Heidegger and Theology*, Vol. I in the series 'New Frontiers in Theology', ed. by James M. Robinson and John B. Cobb, Jr., New York, 1963. The introductory essay by James Robinson gives an illuminating and informative account of the German discussion.

[2] Cf. Gilbert Ryle and others, *The Revolution in Philosophy*, London and New York, 1956; G. J. Warnock, *English Philosophy since 1900*, London, 1958.

regarded as an unclean thing amongst English philosophers and German theologians. From the point of view of English empiricism the thinking of the later Heidegger drips with metaphysics, while from the Heideggerian standpoint the positivist thinking of the English empiricists is not real or primal thinking at all, but stands only on the secondary level of old-time metaphysics which tried to find truth by objectifying conceptualizations, or of science which seeks to provide information, or technology which is mere 'know-how'.[1]

For the later Heidegger primal thinking is concerned with being, which after 1929 gradually came to assume the place occupied by nothing in his earlier philosophy. Anxiety arises from *Dasein's* awareness of being suspended over the abyss of nothingness; this nothing in its turn gives rise to the recognition of the great ontological miracle, namely, that beings are, and not nothing. Thus, nothing becomes 'the veil of being' and the unveiling of being becomes the actual occurrence of being, for being is an event, not a static metaphysical objectivization. It is not *Dasein* which thinks its way through to an underlying metaphysical substance, the 'ultimate reality', or something of that kind. On the contrary, it is being which moves towards *Dasein*, gives itself to *Dasein*, reveals itself to *Dasein*, speaks with 'the voice of being' and in thus addressing 'beings' reveals them as themselves being. Truth is not separate from the occurrence of

[1] The parochial character of philosophy today is most conspicuous: the old post-Reformation saying *cuius regio eius religio* now gives pride of place to *cuius regio eius philosophia*. Heidegger himself never seems to lift his eyes beyond Europe and he never notices the Hebraic character and inspiration of some of his own distinctive ideas. For him the 'path of thought' is a fore-ordained ('fateful') line from Plato to Nietzsche; this seems to follow from his preconceived notion of what metaphysics is, namely, a necessary stage in the transition *via* subject-object conceptualizing ('metaphysics') to the intuitive understanding of being as the event of the revealing of itself as being and not nothing.

being (that is, being), because it is in the event of revealing itself that being is; Heidegger supports this contention by claiming that the original Greek word for 'truth', *alctheia*, literally means 'unveiling', 'disclosure' (*a-letheia*, from the root of *lanthano*, to remain hidden, or to forget). Metaphysics, from Plato onwards, like science and technology, is a forgetting of being, not a disclosure of it; it searches for a 'ground' outside beings themselves (e.g., matter, spirit, God, etc.), and since Descartes the subject has tended to objectivize itself in a concept such as 'ultimate being' or 'reality'. But being is not a being, over against beings; it is what takes place in the event of disclosure, not an ultimate reality which can be grasped by beings. In this way Heidegger considers that his thought has 'overcome' metaphysics.

This inadequate summary of Heidegger's later thought cannot do justice to the insights which are concealed amidst the difficult complications of his language. We are not, however, chiefly concerned with his philosophy as such, but rather with some of the implications for theology which have been discerned in it. From a British point of view it is hardly philosophy at all, but then Heidegger would reply that British empirical philosophy is only the kind of secondary thinking which he has transcended. He himself speaks of his later thought as having taken a 'step backwards', that is, having gone behind the conceptualizing processes of metaphysical and scientific reasoning to that primitive intuition of being which was recognized by the ancient Greeks who first called truth an unveiling. It will seem to many that Heidegger has abandoned philosophy for poetic or mystical vision; but all philosophy in the grand manner starts from an intuition, a 'blik', and rationalizes it. Heidegger's later vision seems to have delivered him from the sadness and futility which pervade the pessimistic existentialist analysis of *Being and Time*.

Heidegger insists that being is not God. On the other

hand, he remarks that he has left open the possibility of a non-metaphysical God, and at the conference of Old Marburgers in 1959 he challenged the theologians to do something about it.[1] To some it might seem that Heidegger has answered Bonhoeffer's call for 'a non-religious interpretation of biblical categories', even though his later thinking is profoundly religious and mystical. What Heidegger in fact does is to provide modern man with a secular parody of the Christian religion. Instead of God he speaks of being; instead of a revelation through the word of God he gives us the disclosure of being through the voice of being. Instead of faith we have primal thinking. Instead of Christ we read of man as 'the shepherd of being'.[2] Instead of a once-for-all victory over sin and death there is the individually repeated salvation from the dread of nothingness and from the futility of secondary thinking and unauthentic existence. Instead of the community of the redeemed there is a gnostic collection of individual primal thinkers. Instead of the fulfilment of man's destiny as the goal of history (eschatology) there is only a disclosure or 'event' of being. Will such twentieth-century gnostic speculation satisfy Bonhoeffer's demand for a non-religious interpretation of biblical categories for the benefit of men come of age? The mild remark of one of the American contributors to the symposium on the later Heidegger seems appropriate here: 'It courts the danger of gratifying modern man's immature religiousness rather than calling him to responsibility.'[3]

[1] Cf. James M. Robinson in *The Later Heidegger and Theology*, op. cit., 34; also Arnold B. Come, ibid., 118.

[2] Heidegger's insistence that being is not God has been likened to Samuel Beckett's insistence that Godot is not God. But it might be noted that, whereas the Christ-motif is implicit in *Waiting for Godot*, there is no Christ-motif at all in Heidegger. Even Tillich retains Christ as 'the New Being', though its historical identification with Jesus is uncertain. For the Christian significance of Godot see Kathleen M. Baxter, *Speak What We Feel*, London, 1964, 9–19.

[3] Carl Michalson in *The Later Heidegger*, 155.

The New Hermeneutics

The Hermeneutic Problem

At first sight it might seem odd that Heidegger's secular interpretation of the biblical categories should have promoted a vigorous discussion amongst theologians. Nevertheless it has helped, or perhaps driven, them to rethink their presuppositions in the light of what he has to say about language as the voice of being. Even though in the last resort primal thinking consists for Heidegger in wordless intuition rather than in articulate speech, authentic language, such as the poets use, is nothing other than being itself speaking through man. This is what is meant when Heidegger asserts that language is the voice of being, or that man does not create language but that language creates man. Speech is what differentiates man from the fauna and flora; authentic speaking, the result of primal thinking, is what distinguishes the authentic person from the unauthentic masses, who are content with chatter, hearsay and the repetition of clichés and second-hand opinion. Man is not fully man (authentic man) until he speaks his own original (primal) thoughts, or, rather, until he becomes the mouthpiece and shepherd of being, so that being speaks through him.

Because he takes language so very seriously, Heidegger could not be content with the linguistic analysis of the English empiricist philosophers. They are talking not about authentic speech but about secondary language (metaphysical, scientific, technological, practical, common-sense, etc.). What is needed is not linguistic analysis but hermeneutics, the art of interpreting primary speech as it is found in the poets, mystics and the like. Hermeneutics involves both the science (literary and historical criticism, etc.) and the art (existential understanding) which can make the words of an authentic speaker, ancient or modern, come alive for us, so that the disclosure of being which once took place in him may happen again in us. This is the conception which has stimulated the liveliest discussion in German theological circles since the original 'demythologizing' debate was sparked off by Bultmann's celebrated lecture of 1941.[1]

Hermeneutics[2] has, of course, been a recognized theological discipline since the Middle Ages, and it traditionally meant the interpretation of the divine speech recorded in the Bible by means of the received dogmas of theology. The Reformation did not fundamentally change this conception, although hermeneutics now became interpretation of the Scriptures according to either the Roman or the Protestant understanding of dogma. The rise of the historical criticism of the Bible in the later eighteenth century, however, made necessary a 'new hermeneutic', because it could no longer be assumed that all the parts of the Bible were equally inspired. Accordingly we find F. D. E. Schleiermacher (1768-1834) supplying a new kind of 'psychological' hermeneutic.[3] Hermeneutics now became not the tortuous elucidation of obscure biblical oracles according to received dogmas, but the projection of the interpreter into the experience of the ancient writer so that he could relive past experience (so Wilhelm Dilthey, 1833-1911). Thus, inevitably, we come to Rudolf Bultmann and the existentialist theology, which dispenses with dogma (and therefore with dogmatic or systematic theology) altogether: hermeneutics, the existen-

[1] Reprinted under the title 'The New Testament and Mythology' in *Kerygma and Myth*, I, Eng. trans. by R. H. Fuller, London, 1953; New York, 1961.

[2] Or hermeneutic: the distinction is immaterial (cf. ethics and ethic). There is only one form in German, *Hermeneutik*. Cf. the Editors' Preface to *The New Hermeneutic*, Vol. II in the series 'New Frontiers in Theology' ed. by James M. Robinson and John B. Cobb, Jr., ixf., New York, 1964. James Robinson's essay, 'Hermeneutic since Barth', pp. 1–77, is the most lucid summary of the whole discussion for English readers.

[3] Cf. R. R. Niebuhr, *Schleiermacher on Christ and Religion*, New York, 1964; London, 1965, 77–91.

tialist interpretation of the Bible, is the whole of theology.[1]
In the hermeneutic task of elucidating the scriptural understanding of human existence we find our understanding of
our own existence changed, and therewith our existence
itself is transformed and we become authentic beings. It is an
axiom of Bultmann's thinking that a change in our understanding of our existence is a change of our existence itself.
Existentialist self-understanding is thus the keynote of his
hermeneutic.

The New Hermeneutic

Bultmann's younger disciples, notably Fuchs and Ebeling,
have carried the matter a step further than he himself was
prepared to go. They have made use, as Bultmann would
not, of the thought of 'the later Heidegger' about language
as the voice of being. Ernst Fuchs (born 1903), now Bultmann's successor as Professor of New Testament at Marburg, holds that it is not simply that the interpreter must
bring a 'pre-understanding' (in Bultmann's view, the existentialist analysis of *Being and Time*) to the text which he
then interprets in the light of it, but rather that the interpreter's own self-understanding is itself changed by being
exposed to the text which addresses him. Interpretation is
what happens when the text itself speaks to us, forces a new
understanding of ourselves upon us, and 'demythologizes'
not its own subject-matter but rather the man who is
addressed by it. What happens in this encounter with the
text is a 'language-event', a 'letting being be' at a particular
moment of time: it is not merely a repeating of the words of
the text, nor yet a reliving of the experience of the writer of
the text (Dilthey), but the letting of language speak to me in

[1] Bultmann's essay, 'The Problem of Hermeneutics', in *Glauben und
Verstehen* II, 1952, will be found in an English translation by J. C. G.
Greig in R. Bultmann, *Essays Philosophical and Theological*, London,
1955.

this new moment of time, here and now. This language-event, when it is authentic language, is a saving-event, God's saving word in the present tense. Thus, the historic (*geschichtlich*) Jesus is no merely historical (*historisch*) figure of the past, reconstructed by historians, but is translated by hermeneutic into language that speaks today, language which challenges us to decision, awakens faith and accomplishes salvation. It is not merely the *kerygma* (proclamation) of the Christ-event, divorced from any concern about the historical Jesus (Bultmann), but the actual words and deeds of the historical Jesus which form the authentic language of salvation and which hermeneutic must translate into word-events of our time. Thus, whereas Bultmann's existentialist theology 'dispersed history into the air' (in Mark Pattison's phrase about D. F. Strauss a century before), the new hermeneutic in Fuchs' hands becomes a means of pursuing anew the abandoned quest of the historical Jesus, whose authentic words, which live again in their challenge to us, are to be understood as a commentary upon his deeds—those actions, such as, for example, eating with publicans and sinners, which indicated that God was drawing near to man in his loving mercy and judgment.[1]

Gerhard Ebeling (born 1912), like his close friend Fuchs, had studied under Bultmann, and is now Brunner's successor in the chair at Zürich. For him hermeneutic is the whole of theology and theology is hermeneutic, since its sole task consists in translating the Word spoken in the Bible into the word for today, the word which can awaken faith amongst non-religious men who have come of age.[2] Man's nature is

[1] Cf. Fuchs, *Hermeneutik*, Bad Constatt, 1954 (2nd ed. 1958); also his contributions to *The New Hermeneutic*, op. cit., especially his 'Response to the American Discussion', 232–43; and his *Studies of the Historical Jesus*, Eng. trans., London, 1964.

[2] Ebeling's *Wort und Glaube* is translated into English as *Word and Faith* by J. W. Leitch, London, 1963; his preoccupation with Bonhoeffer's concern is manifest in many of the essays in this volume. His work on *The Nature of Faith*, Eng. trans. by R. Gregor Smith.

essentially linguistic and hence theology, which is concerned with the Word or address of God to man, must necessarily be hermeneutic. It follows, too, that hermeneutic is not simply a matter of the exposition of the text, the interpreter speaking, but is the process through which the text speaks to us. It is concerned not so much with the understanding of language (though all the philological and critical disciplines are involved), but with understanding *through* language. Language itself speaks; the word interprets itself; the interpreter listens, and it is *his* understanding which is changed. This change, if understanding takes place, is the awakening or renewal of faith; in the interpretation of the Bible there is no understanding without faith, because, if faith is not present, no understanding takes place. When understanding occurs, a 'word-event' has taken place, for the occurrence is always a happening at a certain time; it is not that we rationally apprehend an eternal truth (*logos*, word, in the Greek sense) but that the word lays hold of us in the here and now. Word (cf. Hebrew *dabar*) is 'happening word'. An authentic word is always an event, which, like other significant events, alters the course of the events which follow. The authentic word, because it corresponds to man's destiny, is the word by which one man can speak God to another; it is the word of preaching, authentic preaching which is not hearsay or second-hand, but is the making to occur for men today of the word-events of the biblical texts, supremely, of course, the word and the words of Christ, who is the one, true, authentic word-event. The preacher's 'text' thus becomes a hermeneutical aid in the understanding of present experience. Thus, theological hermeneutic covers all the

London, 1961; Philadelphia, 1962, is an attempt to explain Christian faith to a lay audience. His essay 'Word of God and Hermeneutic' appears in Leitch's translation of *Word and Faith* (305–32) and in *The New Hermeneutic* (ed. Robinson and Cobb, op. cit.), 78–110. He also contributed the important article *Hermeneutik* in *Religion in Geschichte und Gegenwart*, III, 242–62.

theological disciplines. It starts with philology and criticism and it ends with the sermon and with the Christian life (ethics); its task is to translate the speech of the Bible into the word for our own time.[1]

When Words are Events

Fuchs and Ebeling do not make easy reading for the English-speaking world. Their thought is massively Germanic, steeped in Continental theological idiom and full of existentialist jargon. What will the ordinary English reader make of phrases like 'openness to the future', which abound at every turn? Despite the excellence of the translations of Leitch and others, we still need a 'hermeneut' to interpret to us what they are saying, with all the entailed risks of misinterpretation. (How much more true is this of Heidegger himself!) Yet they are saying something very important. If it is true that modern thought advances through the dialogue of philosophy with theology, their work is likely to be significant. The study of hermeneutics today is increasingly recognized as of great importance, not only in philosophy and theology (though it was originally initiated by theology), but also in all the humanities and among the sciences

[1] Space forbids comment upon the attempt of Heinrich Ott (born 1929), Barth's disciple and successor in his chair at Basel, to utilize the thinking of the later Heidegger for the preservation and renewal of dogmatic theology. Barth himself has consistently refused to be entangled with the philosophy of either the earlier or the later Heidegger, remarking wisely that, though everyone must have some sort of philosophy, 'if we do not commit ourselves unreservedly and finally to any specific philosophy, we will not need totally or finally to fear any philosophy' (*Church Dogmatics*, Eng. trans., I, 2, 735). Barth's older disciples, such as Hermann Diem and Walter Schulz, do not look with favour upon Ott's attempt to reconcile Heideggerian philosophy with Barthian theology. See James Robinson's exposition in *The Later Heidegger and Theology*, op. cit. 30–43, and Ott's own essay in the same volume, 'What is Systematic Theology?' 77–111; also his *Denken und Sein : Der Weg M. Heideggers und der Weg der Theologie*, Zürich, 1959.

themselves, where the difficulties of communication, even amongst scientists, are a major stumbling-block to the progress of knowledge. The dialogue between theology and secular (or general) hermeneutics should prove most fruitful in the coming years. It was, after all, in the sphere of biblical studies that critical thinking in the second half of the eighteenth century gave rise to modern historiographical methods as practised by secular historians today;[1] a century hence it may be considered that the permanent significance of Heidegger lies in the fact that he recognized the importance of man's linguisticality and thereby gave fresh impetus to the study of hermeneutics as the basic human intellectual enquiry. If that should prove to be the case, Fuchs and Ebeling will be accorded their due place in the history of ideas, because they recognized the importance of what Heidegger was saying and entered into discussion with him.

But the debate, if it is to become more fruitful, must go beyond its present limited Germanic ambience and become more critical of Heidegger than Fuchs and Ebeling seem to be. Dialogue does not push forward the progress of thought unless it develops by antithesis the ideas of a seminal thinker. Heidegger, after all, is a thinker within a Christian civilization, and what he has done is to take fundamental biblical insights, which had been obscured by positivist 'scientific' thinking, and secularize them. In the process he has reminded theologians brought up in a positivist climate of opinion of something that they ought not to have forgotten. It is ironical that a secular philosopher was needed to re-call Christian thinkers to the recognition of the truth of the biblical doctrine of words and the word of God. Heidegger's 'silent tolling of being', his 'new 'understanding of man as

[1] Cf. Herbert Butterfield, *Man on his Past: a study of the History of Historical Scholarship*, Cambridge and New York, 1954, 26–58; Alan Richardson, *History Sacred and Profane*, London and Philadelphia, 1964, 118–24.

the spokesman of being, is only a secularized restatement of the biblical view of words as defining man's nature in relation to God and neighbour. Heidegger, much more thoroughly than Tillich or Bultmann, has provided 'men come of age' with a non-religious interpretation of biblical categories; and the popular purveyors of 'the new theology' have not yet perceived that he has done their work for them, dispensing altogether with the word 'theology' and with the idea of God. But Heidegger's secular restatement of the biblical doctrine of the word has left out precisely that which has made the Bible everything it has meant for human thought and progress, namely, its speaking about God.

Heidegger himself looks to Hellenic mythology rather than to biblical history as the ground of his hermeneutic; it is the legendary gods and heroes of the Greek poets who are types of his 'voice of being' and who reveal the secrets of the universe. In Greek mythology Hermes was the messenger of the gods, the bearer of divine secrets, and he was credited with the invention of language and with the mastery of the art of interpretation (*hermēneia*[1]). Along with the mythologists—no wonder poor Bultmann was dismayed by this 'step backwards'!—Heidegger sets the poets, notably the German religious poet Hölderlin (1770-1843), in the position of chief interpreters of the mystery of being. The poet is the true priest of mankind, the spokesman of being, who mediates the saving mystery to those who hear his voice. Hence follows all the mystification, lapsing finally into pre-rational wordlessness, which envelops the utterance of the later Heidegger in a cloud of unknowing. Everything is finally engulfed in the ocean of subjectivity. If the poets themselves

[1] In the New Testament the word occurs in I Cor. 12.10 and 14.26 of the interpretation of tongues, etc. St Paul is teaching that it is not the enthusiastic utterance of words which is important, but their interpretation. It is noteworthy that in Acts 14.12 the Lystrans called Paul Hermes (Mercury) 'because he was the chief speaker'.

are the 'hermeneuts', who is to interpret them, and who is to criticize Heidegger's judgment of Hölderlin? Heidegger confuses the expression of poetic or mystic vision with hermeneutics. Who is to say which poet is authentic, or which of the voices of the same poet is his authentic voice?[1]

From this morass of subjectivism Fuchs and Ebeling have effected a partial deliverance by their emphasis upon authentic words as events ('language-event', 'word-event'). But they do not sufficiently stress their character as historical in the sense that they belong to the same history that ordinary secular historians are talking about; for Fuchs and Ebeling *geschichtlich* ('historic') still tends to be understood in the philosophical-existentialist sense of some reality of the past which is independent of actual history (*Historie*) as reconstructed by historians. It is the words of prophets, rather than those of poets and mystics, which are truly historical; this is the emphasis which is lacking in the existentialist theologians, for whom the word or word-event is something which takes place in men's subjectivity or inner consciousness. The authentic word of a prophet, spoken in a crisis of history, is genuinely an historical event; it is a word directed to action, to duty and righteousness, and therefore (in the biblical view) imparts the true knowledge of God (cf. Jer. 22.15f.). We need not go to the Bible to learn this truth, though that is where the doctrine was first enunciated. We may think of Churchill in the crisis of 1940 'mobilizing the resources of the English language' and speaking the authentic word of duty in an hour of decision. Words are indeed events, because they change the whole course of history by

---

[1] Cf. J. K. Stephen's *Lapsus Calami:*

> 'Two voices are there: one is of the deep;
> . . . .
> And one is of an old half-witted sheep
> Which bleats articulate monotony,
> . . . .
> And, Wordsworth, both are thine.'

reason of their commanding authenticity. They continue to reverberate down the corridors of history and, as their relevance for new situations is perceived, they refashion the shape of things centuries after they were first spoken.[1] They create and hold together a community which treasures them, feeds on them and lives by them. Old Testament history, continued in the Church and extended to every part of the world, is the classic example of the power of prophetic words to retain their history-shaping edge across the centuries. The failure of the existentialist theology to take proper account of the prophetic history of the Old Testament, despite the excellent work of contemporary Old Testament scholars like W. Eichrodt, supplies the reason why they have had to learn from Heidegger a vital truth which is part of the Christian biblical inheritance.[2] What is lacking in Heidegger is any recognition of the connection between authentic words and the theme of righteousness. His hermeneutic is concerned with aesthetics and the numinous rather than with ethics and the biblical sense of the holy. Music or painting might be made the voice of being in just the same way as poetic utterance is said to be. The distinctive authenticity of prophecy lies in its concern for righteousness, and in this concern it speaks the challenging and compelling word, not of a nameless, characterless, faceless, anonymous being, but of the God of righteousness who meets men in their awareness of his demand for righteousness and speaks to them his name. 'To hear' and 'to obey' are near synonyms in the Old Testament and the knowledge of God comes by doing his

[1] Cf. *Magna Carta*, of which the words did not originally convey to those who first used them the significance which has subsequently been found in them.

[2] Cf. Bultmann's essay on 'The Significance of the Old Testament for the Christian Faith' in *Glauben und Verstehen* I (1933), reprinted in Bernhard W. Anderson (ed.), *The Old Testament and Christian Faith* (New York, 1963; London, 1964), and the various contributions to this volume. One may note in it the frequency of the occurrence of the word 'Marcionite'.

will. Theology and ethics are one subject, not two. Many who are concerned about personal righteousness and social justice are not as ignorant of God as they might themselves suppose. In Hebraic thought sonship is calculated in terms of obedience to a father's will (cf. Matt. 21.28-31), and speaking about the Sonship of Jesus is a way of emphasizing the ethical character of Christology. The obedient Son, whose actions authenticate his words, is most fittingly described in the New Testament as the Word of God—the 'word-event' which affects the course of all history, whether of the individual man or of the world.

There is no higher Christological category than that of the Word of God, if we keep within the framework of biblical thought. The prophets had demonstrated the power of authentic words in the great crises of Israel's history and their utterance was destiny-laden. Their words were not their own: not 'being', but the God who demands righteousness, was speaking through them. Because they were speaking about righteousness, enunciating the will of God in a particular historical crisis, they could declare with confidence, 'Thus saith the Lord'. They knew that their words, because they were not 'mere words', not even merely their own words, had a dread self-fulfilling efficacy; the word of the Lord would not return to him void, but would accomplish that whereunto it was sent (cf. Isa. 55.10f.). It was in this prophetic act of enunciating the will of God in particular concrete situations that the knowledge of God was received in Israel. The prophets of Israel wrote great poetry, greater than Hölderlin's, but it was not because of its poetic quality that it spoke and still speaks to men about God; it was because it spoke about obedience that it unveiled the mystery of God. The authentic character of words is tested in action and in result, not simply in the existential experience of individual hearers: by their fruits ye shall know them. It is in the concretely historical character of the word of righteousness, not merely in the existentialist-*geschichtlich* sense, but in actual historical situations like the invasion of Palestine by Assyria or Babylon, that the authentic word of the prophet discloses itself as the word of God. It was because of their experience of the word of God in history, in all its self-realizing and overriding potency, that the prophets of Israel came to formulate the doctrine of the creation of the world by the word of God. Nature itself, the whole cosmos, which is the theatre of the history in which God speaks to the prophets, is brought into being and providentially ordered by the creative and redeeming Word of God: 'The word of the Lord is right, and all his work is done in faithfulness. He loveth righteousness and judgment; the earth is full of his loving kindness. By the word of the Lord were the heavens made, and all the host of them by the breath of his mouth. . . . Let all the earth fear the Lord; let all the inhabitants of the world stand in awe of him; for he spake and it was done, he commanded and it stood fast. . . .' (Ps. 33.4-9). The doctrine of the God who rules history and nature by his word is the least mythological and the least anthropomorphic way in which the relationship of God and the world ('creation') can be spoken about. No imagery derived from the craft of a man working with his hands, such as Plato's myth of the Demiurge in the *Timaeus*, is adequate, because the biblical idea of God as the Creator of all things, unlike the images of the heathen gods, is derived from the prophetic experience of the miracle that men can themselves speak the words of God and know something of their authentic, self-fulfilling potency. It is through the prophet's obedient hearing that the word of God discloses itself under the species of human words.

The New Hermeneutics

SUGGESTIONS FOR FURTHER READING

There is not yet in English a wide choice of reading on this subject. Undoubtedly the most helpful books are those mentioned in the footnotes above, Vols. I and II in the series 'New Frontiers in Theology' edited by James M. Robinson and John B. Cobb and published by Harper and Row, New York. The works of Fuchs and Ebeling which have been translated (also mentioned above) should be consulted. A useful general introduction to Heidegger is Magda King's *Heidegger's Philosophy: A Guide to his Basic Thought*, Oxford (Blackwell) and New York, 1964.

6

THE DEATH OF GOD: A REPORT
EXAGGERATED

MARK TWAIN, when he heard that the American newspapers had printed his obituary notice, cabled from Europe to the Associated Press: 'The reports of my death are greatly exaggerated'. It is now some eighty years since Friedrich Nietzsche (1844-1900) announced the death of God; yet in his tortured soul he knew that he as anti-Christ could be pagan not in the old Greek sense but only as a kind of Christian pagan. In *Zarathustra* the 'last Pope', having become redundant now that God was dead, declares that some God must have converted him to his godlessness. In our own century many lesser Nietzsches (such as D. H. Lawrence) have sought the old, genuine paganism, but have found only a post-Christian version which is unthinkable without a Christian background. If they proclaimed that God was dead, they did so in unconscious revolt from the insipid and evaporated Christianity of their day, which offered to men not the strong, holy, living God of the Bible who comes forth to meet them in their need, but a demythologized God who resides only in the 'depth' of their own shallow being. Feuerbach (1804-72) and the theologians who 'interpreted' him to the educated public a century ago made Nietzsche and Lawrence inevitable by their teaching that 'God' was only that aspect of our encounter with our own self in the depth of our being which brings us to true self-awareness ('the Self-Confronting Essence of the Mind').

102

Such a God is not the living God of biblical faith, but is already a dead God; if the report of the death of God is based on nothing more than the theories of Feuerbach and his successors, it will turn out to be greatly exaggerated. It is curious that the 'radical' religious-atheistic thinking of the twentieth century has not so far significantly advanced beyond the thought of the nineteenth. It strikes many people in our generation as novel and exciting only because they know nothing of the development of European thought in the century of Feuerbach and Nietzsche.

Can we Prove the Existence of God?

Ought we to expect to be able to prove God's existence? A short period of reflection will convince us that the word 'proof' is not very helpful in this discussion. In its strict sense proof is possible only in very limited areas of human thinking, such as pure mathematics and pure logic. The word 'proof' in this sense would be relevant only in connection with a very abstract definition of God, such as 'that than which nothing greater can be conceived' (as St Anselm well knew). No existential commitment on our part, no trust, obedience or worship would be involved. A God capable of proof or disproof would be the 'God' of metaphysics, a being whose existence would depend upon human reasoning, not the God upon whom both we and our reasoning alike depend.

Sometimes the word 'proof' is used loosely of demonstrations in the sphere of natural science, as when we might say that physics proves that this heavier stone will not fall faster than that lighter one. Of course, in such contexts we ought to speak of a high degree of inductive probability rather than of proof. But, even so, the area of our human experience in which inductive probability of a scientific kind is attainable is strictly limited and does not include the inner recesses of human personality itself. In the human sciences there is little that corresponds to the inductive probability of the natural sciences; in psychology or the social sciences there are no 'laws' comparable in universality to the law of gravity. In fact, when we have reached the level of personal existence, the word 'proof' is hardly ever applicable; I cannot prove that my friend will not stab me in the back (literally or metaphorically) tomorrow morning: I have to trust him. I may indeed trust him confidently, but I cannot prove to a third party (for example, my lawyer) that he will act as I predict. Friendship has very little to do with inductive probabilities and our personal relationships are not sustained by calculating them.

This brings us to a third (and very old) use of the word 'prove': the acquiring of confidence in something (or someone) by making personal trial of its (or his) dependability. In this sense the word is used a great deal in the Bible; a study of it with the aid of a concordance would tell us much about the nature of religious belief. It has three principal uses in connection with God. First, men attempt to prove God, to put him to the test and see whether he is worthy of their trust: this is regarded as unfaith, the gravest sin into which presumptuous men can fall. What happened at Massah (which means 'proving') remained for ever in Hebrew eyes the standing example of the danger of 'testing' (tempting, trying) God (Ex. 17.7 in its context; Deut. 33.8; Pss. 81.7, 95.9; Heb. 3.9); it was not God who was on trial, but Israel. To try to prove God's existence or his fidelity to his word was for the men of the Bible the ultimate sin. They would have uncompromisingly told us that to try to prove God's existence was both sinful and futile (Deut. 8.3; Job 38-41; Eccles. 5.2; Matt. 4.7). It was utter foolishness, and for the Hebrew foolishness was not so much an intellectual defect as a moral one (Ps. 14).

But, secondly, there is a good sense in which men can

prove God: they can trustfully accept his promise and experience his goodness for themselves, so that they do not have to accept his truth second-hand: 'O taste and see how gracious the Lord is; blessed is the man that trusteth in him' (Ps. 34.8).[1] It is to be noted that in such passages the act of trust precedes the experience of the goodness of God; those who will not make the decision of faith will experience nothing. It cannot be too heavily stressed that in the Bible God has already come forward to meet man and that it is for man to make the response; if he asks for further 'proofs', if he demands a 'sign', he will find nothing. As we have already noted, religion in all its forms represents not our quest for God but God's quest for us. Our part in the divine enterprise is that of responding to an invitation and thus proving for ourselves what is the good and acceptable will of God (Rom. 12.2). In this sense by our own decision we can prove the goodness of God (and therefore, quite incidentally, his existence: cf. Heb. 11.6), but this will be a personal or existential proof, not one which is admissible as evidence at the bar of positivist philosophy.

Thirdly, and most characteristically, in the Bible it is God who 'proves' us, not we who prove God. Even though it feels to us from our anthropocentric, pre-biblical standpoint that it is we who are putting God on trial, this is only an illusion of perspective: 'Lord, thou hast searched me out and known me . . . ' (Ps. 139.1). We commit the presumptuous sin of demanding that God shall offer us proofs that his promises are true and even of demanding that he shall furnish us with a certificate of his existence, while all the time he is the one who requires truth in our most inward parts and who alone makes us understand wisdom (Ps. 51.6).

[1] Cf. the Tate and Brady paraphrase (new version) of this verse:

'O make but trial of his love:
Experience will decide
How blest are they, and only they,
Who in his truth confide.'

Why doesn't God Demonstrate His Existence?

The question is sometimes asked why, if God is all-powerful and wants us to believe in him, does he not demonstrate his reality by giving the world a sign which no atheist could misread? Why does he not write his name across the sky so luridly that unbelief would be impossible? To ask such a question at all indicates that the word of God spoken in the prophets and in Christ has not been heard or understood. God would not then be the God who chose the way of the servant in order that he might win the love of men, given freely and uncoerced. Allegiance to a God whose cosmic commercials had broken down man's sales-resistance would be a very different thing from that utter commitment to incarnate love which was elicited from one of the apostles when he cried to his fellow-disciples, 'Let us go with him, that we may die with him' (John 11.16; cf. 13.37). We may doubt, like Thomas, or break down, like Peter; but, when the word which God has addressed to us has truly been heard by us, we know that its claim is the ultimate truth for us (cf. John 6.68). We shall then understand what the expression 'the word of God' means; no longer will we entertain crude mental images of mystical voices which speak shadow words into something which we think of as our inward ears after we have made our minds a blank. God's word is the word he has spoken once for all in Christ, proclaimed beforehand in the Old Testament and affirmed as present in history by the New Testament writers. God's word is Christ, whose story from manger-cradle to criminal's rack and rich man's grave is a true parable of the humility of the divine love, which goes to all lengths to seek and to save that which is lost, but which in the end, because it is love, will not use coercion or cajolery to secure obedience, leaving us free to accept or reject his invitation, free to speculate about his existence or his intentions, free

> To guess from the insulted face
> Just what appearances he saves
> By suffering in a public place
> A death reserves for slaves.[1]

Having done all that love can do, having prepared the welcome and given the sign, God waits for us to come to him, as the father of the Prodigal waited for his son's return. How can prosaic language express this profound demonstration of the humility of the divine love? Small wonder that the language of religion is the language of poetry. George Herbert in 'Christmas' describes the meeting of his soul with the Christ who was all along expecting him, waiting for him, when at last 'the grief of pleasures' should bring him to him:

> O Thou, whose glorious yet contracted light,
>   Wrapt in Night's mantle, stole into a manger,
> Since my dark soul and brutish is thy right
>   To man, of all beasts, be not thou a stranger:
> Furnish and deck my soul, that Thou mayest have
>   A better lodging than a rack or grave.[2]

The answer, therefore, to the question why God does not offer proofs of his existence as the sovereign Lord of all things is that he has in fact done so, but only to those who have understood the true nature of kingship. Divine kingship consists not in coercive power but in patient love. God, because he is God, chooses to win man's love where he could have coerced his assent. To do this involves the humility of making an appeal to those whom he could have commanded. God does not want us to believe in him because we have been overawed by his power or impressed by his

---

[1] W. H. Auden, 'Friday's Child' in *Homage to Clio*, London, Faber, 1958.
[2] *The Oxford Book of Christian Verse*, Oxford and New York, 1940, 154.

wonders; he does not want us to give him our allegiance as a result of our misunderstanding of his true nature, so that we should seek him because we desire the material prosperity that might be assured to us by being on the winning side (cf. John 6.26). He wants us to respond to what he is, not to what he is not, and he is the one who loves without asking for reward and who expects us to serve him by loving other people in the same way. It is precisely because he is the God of *love* that he does not give any other sign than that which he has given in Jesus Christ. Having given that sign, no other sign is necessary: no other sign could add anything to it; no cosmic demonstration, no metaphysical proof, could elicit the kind of faith which God desires. Better a passionate atheist than a fellow-traveller who follows for the wrong reasons; the kingdom of heaven would be overflowing if it contained all those who could be browbeaten or bribed into saying 'Lord, Lord' (cf. Matt. 7.21-3). To seek any other sign is to show that we have not understood the sign which has been given; it is a seeking after a false image of God, which is idolatry (cf. Matt. 16.4).

Hearing and Hearsay

We must distinguish between the faith which comes by hearing (Rom. 10.17) and the assimilation of ideas which come by hearsay. Faith which is man's response to the hearing of the word of Christ is a personal commitment to him as the revelation of the love of God, which created and sustains the world and which sets one free to trust and obey the divine commandment of love. To believe is to hear; to hear is to obey; to obey is to be free to serve the love of God as directed towards our fellow-men (John 15.9-17). Faith is therefore always intimately personal, involving personal attitudes towards one whom we trust and adore. Faith in the Christian sense is belief *in*, not belief *that*, even though it is true that we must always try to articulate our faith in God by means of statements in the form of 'believing that'. If I believe in my doctor or my friend, I would, if challenged to state why I believed in him, go on to analyse the grounds of my trust in the form of belief that: that he has never let me down, that his counsel has always proved valuable in the past, that he is the kind of person who puts himself out to help others, and so on; but I would probably never trouble to analyse my belief if I were not challenged by someone else's questioning to do so. And I would indignantly deny that my faith was self-induced and unsupported by any evidence; I would insist that it was the intrinsic quality of my doctor or my friend which had created my faith in him, not some subjective impressions of my own. So it is with faith in Christ: it is he who has awakened faith in us by being what he was and doing what he did. And when I find that my initial decision to trust in him is confirmed by my actual experience of doing so, then I may say that I have 'proved' him and know personally that his word is truth. For now I know that God, thus made present to me in my acknowledgment of Christ's claim upon me, is the one who cannot be denied except by someone who does not know whom or what he is denying.

Contrast this kind of faith, which comes by hearing, with the second-hand faith which comes by hearsay. Let us call this undeliberate form of assent 'second-hand faith'; the technical theological term for it is *fides historica*, the pattern of ideas inherited from the past, a dead faith. It moves wholly within the circle of 'belief that' and never breaks through to the personal dimension of 'belief in'. Second-hand faith is something which has rubbed off on us from contact with parents, teachers and other influences in our formative years. We have accepted it uncritically, but have never really made it our own. So long as we are not challenged, we go on happily without thinking much about it, in just the same way that we go on accepting the conventional ideas of the social group to which we belong, our class, our local community, and so on. We conform to the hearsay standards of 'everyone else' and in time we come to resent anyone who appears to question or deny them. But it may happen one day that we find our inherited assumptions severely challenged; we may, for example, have gone up to the university and found ourselves amongst people whose vocation is to challenge all ill-founded notions of every kind, whether secular or religious; or we might begin to study philosophy and learn about the verification principle; or we might listen to some 'humanist' speaker on the radio explaining that modern cosmology has made religion out of date. And then our second-hand faith will prove of no avail; before the flowing tides of the 'new thinking' we shall find ourselves submerged in the ocean of doubt.

Second-hand faith is not really faith at all in the biblical sense. It is mere 'belief that'. It is only a kind of lazy intellectual assent to certain propositions which, though they may be couched in biblical phrases, are actually metaphysical in character. They are stored in the lumber-room of our minds, which we hardly ever visit and have never cleaned out. All of us have such a lumber-room, however scientifically appointed the front rooms of our minds may be. The stuff in the lumber-room (which is pushed there because we never use it) is the accumulated deposit of hearsay belief, ideas about God and human destiny and the like. They are an odd collection of unassorted objects, which we have acquired we know not how. Amongst them there will be sure to be plenty of Victoriana, but most of them will be older still, deistic notions about God from 'the eighteenth century and a good deal of the débris of the shattered mediaeval world picture, the three-story universe, the saints and the devils, Noah's Ark and Adam's rib. The shadowy God who lurks amongst the lumber is the God of metaphysics, the one who is the co-ordinating principle that could—if only we had time to work it all out—give unity and meaning to everything else. But unfortunately the God of metaphysics proves unable to defend himself as soon as it is pointed out to us that he is only one object amongst others and that he, too, needs accounting for. The hearsay God is not the God of faith, for the God of faith is always the subject who addresses us and cannot be made an object of our conceiving. It is only when we have gone beyond the notional God of indirect speech that we become aware of one whose reality does not require or permit of proof. At this point we shall have passed from hearsay to hearing, and we shall deplore our former heedlessness and conventionality. We shall know what is meant when, after all his lengthy arguments about the goodness of God, God himself speaks and Job declares, 'I had heard of thee by the hearing of the ear, but now mine eye sees thee; therefore I despise myself and repent in dust and ashes' (Job 42.5f.).[1]

It is a commonplace of television religious discussions that there has been a large-scale decline in religious belief during the last few decades. ('Wouldn't you agree, Archbishop, that a great number of people nowadays no longer believe in God?') The disservice to clear thinking which is done by such discussions arises from the fact that a frequently repeated shibboleth sinks comfortably into drowsy minds, which are naturally prone to accept hearsay and in due course pass it on. No radical questioning is aroused and new hearsay notions fill the vacuum left by the passing of the old ones. The important point to notice is that it is not genuine Christian belief, the faith which comes by hearing, which is declining; it is the *fides historica* of the unauthentic multitudes which is fading away.

[1] These are properly the concluding words of the Book of Job; the remaining verses (42.7–17) constitute the attempt of a later editor to give the poem a happy ending.

This semi-Christianized, largely mediaeval, hotch-potch of inherited ideas is slowly dissolving under the impact of the modern scientific world view, as it filters slowly down to the masses; but it is probable that the disintegration is being even more effectively hastened by the dawning of the results of the theological revolution of the last hundred years. The vague assumptions of Victorian *fides historica* are at last beginning to crumble: the accepted metaphysical idea of God as the first cause, the anthropomorphic notions of him as our grandfather in heaven, the superstitious veneration of the Bible as a literalistically inspired book of divine oracles, the old three-story cosmology, antiquated ideas of hell and heaven—all these things, which, of course, were never authentic elements of Christian theology, are now clearly on their way out of the mental lumber-room of the people of the Western world. We can call this process of disintegration a decline of religious belief, if we like; we can speak of it as a sign of man's coming of age, if that is what it seems to us to be; but we cannot seriously speak of it as a decline in genuine Christian belief. We have little reason to lament it; the disappearing world of metaphysical half-belief was nothing more than a penumbra of shadows which seemed light only in comparison with the total darkness of absolute agnosticism and unbelief. We ought to be grateful to the linguistic philosophers who are helping to clear it out of the way. It is doubtful whether in fact the number of genuine Christian believers in the Western world today is smaller than it was a century ago, when Victorian class-consciousness demanded an outward conformity to the conventions of religious observance as a condition of the recognition of one's social respectability. Not having to acknowledge beliefs which one does not hold, and not having to go to church because of social pressures, are perhaps two twentieth-century concessions to the indubitably Christian virtue of being honest to God.

The Death of God: A Report Exaggerated

Grace and Anti-grace

The fundamental character of man is freedom. Not to be free is to be less than human. Animals, even wild animals, are not free in the human way; they are controlled by instincts and impulses which they do not understand. What is intolerable about grinding poverty, economic drudgery or totalitarian regimentation is that these things limit the area of human freedom and so deprive their victims of their essential humanity. No one, of course, is absolutely free; we cannot reverse the consequences of our actions if we defy the laws of gravity or of health, and we are subject to restraint if we offend against the laws of the society in which we live. Indeed, in the conditions of human life freedom is possible only within a framework of law, whether the laws of nature or the laws of society. But the supreme object of law in the sense of social legislation is to preserve and increase the area of individual human freedom. The recognition of this truth is society's acknowledgment that the basic fact about man is his freedom. Non-Christian philosophers, such as Aristotle or Confucius, have long perceived that the basic human problem is the problem of freedom. Christian theology has insisted that God's dealings with mankind are subordinated to his solicitude for human freedom; he yearns for the trust and obedience of his creatures, but only if they are freely given to him: coerced loyalty and obedience (as every parent or teacher knows) are not loyalty and obedience at all. Christian affirmations of respect for human personality are grounded upon belief in God's regard for human freedom as an essential aspect of his love.

To deprive a person of his freedom is to dehumanize him because it diminishes his responsibility. To be human is to be responsible for one's own choices and to accept responsibility. The unauthentic masses who take their opinions from hearsay and conform their behaviour to the standards of the faceless people around them are not in the deeper sense either responsible or free; to them freedom means nothing more than doing what one likes. True freedom consists in taking responsibility for moral decisions. Probably all human choices are moral ones; it may seem that whether I should take my holiday in Scarborough or Dunoon hardly involves a moral issue, but then there is always the question whether I should take a holiday at all, so that I could give more to Oxfam. In any case, even when we are making our most ordinary choices in daily life, we are none of us as free as we might suppose we are. We are all of us subject to the influences, good and bad, which flow in upon us from the social environment around us, so that even when we think that our choice is our own, we are really yielding, perhaps quite unconsciously, to the pressures of the society around us which forces us into its mould. It is not at all easy for a person to be free, responsible and human; it is so much easier to be conformed, malleable and unauthentic. We are truly human only in so far as we take our moral experience seriously.

By moral experience is meant our awareness of a pressure upon us to do what we think is right. This pressure may be due in some measure to early education, social conditioning, and so on; but it cannot be explained away entirely in terms of social conditioning, for otherwise we could not account for the appearance of truly authentic men, like Socrates or Amos, who break away from the conventional standards and practices of their generation and create new ideals of social behaviour. It is true that all our conceptions of what is right are partly conditioned by environmental factors, and our very ideals are always subject to rational criticism; but to be human is to *know* that there is a difference between right and wrong and to feel a sense of unease if we do not choose the right ('conscience'). Furthermore, we know that our ideals and such attainments as we have achieved are not really our own; if we are honest with ourselves, we will admit that they are the result of good influences which have been exercised upon us by others whom we admire and by the society, nation, school, family, and so on, to which we have belonged. A person who attributes moral achievement to himself is a prig. On the other hand, though we are always tempted to blame our moral failures upon others or upon 'society' (which threatens us with nuclear extinction and so disintegrates our personalities), we know in our heart that we ought not to have yielded to bad influences and that modern people, come of age, have no excuse for objectifying the evil in their lives in the form of a personal Devil, or their 'environment' or anything else.

What we have been discussing (though in secular language) is the Christian doctrine of grace. What is it which, against our inclination, our self-interest and even our social conditioning, makes us do (or at least want to do) what is right? It is always to some extent a power outside ourselves. This outside influence is what theologians have traditionally called grace, but it is something which we all experience in our daily lives. I am influenced by my friend, or by the high standards of some group to which I belong. We are all of us recipients of daily grace; otherwise we would not be moral beings at all. Strongest of all is the grace of love, which enables us to become what the person who loves us, or whom we love, wants us to be. It is this *enabling* power which is of the essence of grace, the power which makes us able to be what we could not have become by our own efforts. 'The grace of the Lord Jesus Christ' has been an historical fact, attested again and again by men and women who have changed the course of history, and who have all asserted that it was not their own strength which enabled them to be what they became and to do what they did. The curious thing about grace is that, because it attracts but does not compel, it resolves the conflict between determinism and free-will, so that we feel most completely free when we have surrendered our wills most completely to another. 'My will is not mine own, till it is wholly thine.' This is the deepest aspect of human responsibility, the achievement of the obedience of sons to the Lord whose service is perfect freedom; but it is not without analogies in our everyday relationships with other people.

There is, however, another reality, which might be called anti-grace. We are all of us recipients of daily anti-grace; it flows in upon us at all times; we absorb it, often unconsciously, from the low tone of the society around us, from the papers we read and the unauthentic triviality (and worse) which is daily poured into our homes by radio and television, from the hearsay opinions of the company we keep, from the example of those who have demonstrated the advantages of being men of the world by their ability to get on in it. We can surrender our wills to the anti-grace of a secularized and immoral society; we can, in extreme situations, surrender our human freedom to a Hitler or some other demagogue. St Paul has a good deal to say about being slaves to sin, and the consequent illusions of freedom which are only the veil of servitude. He tells us that by becoming slaves of Christ, we are set free from the bondage of the world and thus to grow to the fulness of the stature of the sons of God, which is our true human birthright and our adult human status. The choice is ours. At least, that is what it feels like at the time. But after we have made it, we come to realize that the choice, though ours, was really our response to one who was choosing us and enabling us to make the decision which we could not ourselves have carried through. And this is what is meant by the grace of God through Jesus Christ our Lord.

The Death of God: A Report Exaggerated

Beyond Humanism

One suspects that the real issue between Christians and humanists turns upon the doctrine of grace and only afterwards becomes a question about the existence of God. It is first and foremost a question about man, his status, freedom and destiny. Where do all the good impulses in human nature come from? Whence all the readiness to find and serve the truth, to banish ignorance and superstition, to seek a just and equal social order, to destroy the ugly and create the beautiful—all those things for which the genuine humanist is so passionately concerned? Are they simply the products of a merely human longing and nothing more? And why are they frustrated at every turn, so that human nature which conceives and desires these ends is so impotent to bring them to fulfilment? Has unaided human nature the resources within itself to triumph over anti-grace? The genuine Christian will doubtless answer these questions by looking into his own heart. He will acknowledge that by himself he can do nothing, that his own resources are unequal to the conquest of anti-grace, and that apart from grace the issue must inevitably be settled in favour of despair. Hope is possible for him because he has experienced what the power of the divine grace has done for him. And, having made trial of that power, he has come to recognize the grace of God at work in the hearts of many humanist lovers of truth and beauty and goodness who have not yet themselves learned to identify the source of the inspiration of their lives. The whole life of men, in so far as they are in earnest about truth and value, is permeated by 'prevenient' grace, even though they may perhaps not know it. Grace, divine aid, is not something confined to the narrow ambience of men's 'ecclesiastical' lives; grace is not 'churchy'. As Karl Rahner has said, 'Just because grace is free and unmerited, this does not mean that it is rare (theology has been led

117

astray for too long already by the tacit assumption that grace would no longer be grace if God became too free with it).'[1]

God's grace is not rare. We can never too zealously praise God for the covenanted mercies of his grace in the Bible and the sacraments of the Church, but we fall into grievous error if we suppose that his grace is limited only to the ecclesiastical sphere. Grace is all around us every day. Countless men and women, faithfully performing the duties of their secular occupations and indeed often going far beyond the requirements of those duties in their patient service of their fellow human beings, are inspired and sustained by daily grace, even though they do not know it, or only half-know it. The doctrine of grace is the heart and centre of the Christian religion, and indeed from the Christian point of view the grace of God is the source of origin of all the world's religions. For the heart of man as such is moved as by a magnet towards him in whom all values meet and all human aspiration finds its fulfilment.

When we speak of God as personal, we do not imply that he is subject to the limitations which human personality necessarily involves; we mean that our analogies of God's action upon our hearts must be drawn from the sphere of our deepest and most satisfying human personal relationships, in which a genuine accord of wills implies unity without coercion and surrender without subservience. No analogies from cybernetics can ever be adequate; they confuse the issue by raising unreal theoretical problems about determinism and freewill. No analysis in terms of anxiety or dread (*Angst*) can ever adequately describe the human condition. The Christian insight into that condition must be expressed in terms of restlessness, discontent with all that man can achieve or possess until our hearts rest in God; and

---

[1] Karl Rahner, *Nature and Grace*, London and New York, 1963, 31.

this condition is itself a token of the divine love.[1] In his wisdom the God of love so made man that, if the values and riches of the world failed to draw him to the source of all good, then at last weariness and dissatisfaction would bring him to his true home. So George Herbert in his poem 'The Pulley' pictures God as having lavished upon man all riches and values and pleasures, but finally withholding the supreme gift of rest, satisfaction or fulfilment: the other blessings man may keep and enjoy, but the gift of contentment must be withheld for man's own good:

> Yet let him keep the rest,
> But keep them with repining restlessness;
> Let him be rich and weary, that at last,
> If goodness lead him not, yet weariness
> May toss him to my breast.[2]

SUGGESTIONS FOR FURTHER READING

Karl Barth, *From Rousseau to Ritschl*, Eng. trans., London and New York, 1959, esp. chap. IX (Feuerbach).

Karl Löwith, *From Hegel to Nietzsche: the Revolution in Nineteenth Century Thought*, Eng. trans., New York, 1964; London, 1965 (for advanced study).

John Baillie, *Our Knowledge of God*, Oxford and New York, 1939.

Karl Rahner, *Nature and Grace*, Eng. trans., Stagbooks, London and New York, 1963.

Emil Brunner, *Truth as Encounter*, Philadelphia and London, 1964: new and enlarged edition of *Wahrheit als Begegnung*, Zurich, 1938.

[1] Cf. the profound saying of St Augustine. 'Thou hast made us for thyself, and our heart is restless (*inquietum*) till it rests in thee' (*Confessions* I, i. 1).

[2] *The Oxford Book of Christian Verse*, 155.

Helmut Gollwitzer, *The Existence of God as Confessed by Faith*, Eng. trans., London and Philadelphia, 1965 (for advanced study).

Wallace I. Matson, *The Existence of God*, Cornell University Press, Ithaca, New York and Oxford, 1965.

H. D. Lewis, *Philosophy of Religion*, London, 1965.

Donald M. Baillie, *God was in Christ*, London, 1948; Faber paperback, 1961.

A. T. Hanson, (ed.), *Vindications: Essays on the historical basis of Christianity*, London and New York, 1966.

Lesslie Newbigin, *Honest Religion for Secular Man*, London and Philadelphia, 1966.

David Jenkins, *Guide to the Debate about God*, London and Philadelphia, 1966.

INDEX OF NAMES

INDEX OF NAMES

Agrippa (Herod), 24f.
Alaric the Goth, 22
Amos, 114
Anderson, Bernhard W., 98n.
Andrew, Father, 23
Anselm, St, 103
Aristotle, 31, 69, 113
Asquith, H. H., 20
Auden, W. H., 107
Augustine, St, 35, 119
Ayer, A. J., 56n.

Bacon, Francis, 21
Baillie, D. M., 120
Baillie, John, 32f., 40, 48, 64, 68f., 119
Barth, Karl, 17-21, 26-9, 33, 41n., 84, 94n., 119
Baxter, Kathleen M., 48, 88n.
Beckett, Samuel, 88n.
Beecham, H. Audrey, 80n.
Berkeley, George, 68
Bevan, Edwyn, 80n.
Bismarck, Otto von, 19
Boman, Thorleif, 71f.
Bonhoeffer, D., 19-21, 38, 39n., 41n., 58n., 60n., 84, 88, 92n.
Bousset, W., 18n.
Bradlaugh, Charles, 40
Braithwaite, R. B., 57f.
Braun, Herbert, 55
Brunner, Emil, 84, 92, 119
Bultmann, Rudolf, 39n., 52-4, 60, 70, 75f., 81, 84, 90-2, 96

Buren, Paul van, 39f., 58n., 60
Butler, Joseph, 60
Butterfield, Herbert, 95n.

Calhoun, R. L., 20
Churchill, Sir Winston, 97
Cobb, John B., 85n., 90n., 101
Come, Arnold B., 88n.
Comte, Auguste, 41n.
Colet, John, 41n.
Confucius, 113
Copernicus, 31
Cox, Harvey, 45n., 48
Cyrus, 25

Darwin, Charles, 69
Democritus, 14
Descartes, R., 68, 87
Devlin, Lord, 42
Diem, Hermann, 94n.
Dilthey, Wilhelm, 90f.

Ebeling, Gerhard, 63n., 64, 91-5, 97, 101
Edwards, David L., 29
Eichrodt, Walther, 98
Einstein, Albert, 69
Epicurus, 14, 68
Erasmus, 41n.
Evans, D. D., 58n.

Farrer, Austin, 80n.
Felix, 25

Festus, 24f.
Feuerbach, L. A., 102f., 119
Fuchs, Ernst, 91f., 94f., 97, 101

Gibbon, Edward, 22
Godsey, John D., 29
Gollwitzer, Helmut, 55, 64f., 120
Green, T. H., 68
Gregory VII, Pope, 43

Halmos, Paul, 44n.
Hamilton, Kenneth, 51n.
Hammer, R. J., 48
Hare, R. M., 58n.
Harnack, A. von, 18n.
Heasman, Kathleen, 48
Hegel, G. W. F., 50
Heidegger, M., 15, 52, 67, 78, 81-
    101
Heine, Heinrich, 55
Herbert, George, 107, 119
Hermes, 96
Hesiod, 13f.
Hick, John, 58n., 64
Hinshelwood, Sir Cyril, 67
Hitler, A., 116
Hobbes, Thomas, 68
Holbach, Baron von, 68
Hölderlin, J. C. F., 96f., 99
Hollweg, Bethmann, 19f.
Homer, 13
Hooft, W. A. Visser 't, 28n.

Jarrett-Kerr, Martin, 48
Jenkins, Daniel T., 29

Kant, Immanuel, 69
Keys, Ivor C. B., 80n.
Kierkegaard, S., 52, 56, 82
King, Magda, 101

Laplace, P. S., 69

Lawrence, D. H., 102
Leeuwen, A. T. van, 48
Leitch, J. W., 92n., 94
Leucippus, 68
Lewis, H. D., 120
Lightfoot, J. B., 61n.
Löwith, Karl, 119
Lucretius, 14
Luke, St, 73f., 79

Macquarrie, John, 53n.
Marcel, G., 52
Marty, Martin E., 29
Marx, Karl, 25
Mascall, E. L., 48
Matson, Wallace I., 120
Meynell, Hugo A., 29
Michalson, Carl, 88n.
Moore, P., 48
More, Sir Thomas, 41n.

Niebuhr, H. R., 20
Niebuhr, Reinhold, 20
Niebuhr, R. R., 90n.
Nietzsche, Friedrich, 86n., 102f.

Ogden, Schubert M., 55n.
Oldham, J. H., 20
Ott, Heinrich, 94n.

Pascal, Blaise, 34, 69f.
Pattison, Mark, 92
Paul, St, 24, 34, 61, 96n., 116
Paul, Pope, 43
Pilate, Pontius, 25, 76
Plato, 13, 68, 86n., 87, 100
Polycarp, 61
Ptolemy of Alexandria, 69

Rahner, Karl, 117f., 119
Ramsey, Ian T., 58n., 80n.
Raven, Charles E., 20

Index of Names

Reitzenstein, R., 18n.
Richardson, Alan, 19n., 48, 53n., 73n., 76n., 80, 95n.
Robertson, F. W., 37
Robinson, James M., 85n., 88n., 90n., 94n., 101
Robinson, J. A. T., 19n., 65
Russell, (Lord) Bertrand, 14f., 60, 68
Ryle, Gilbert, 85n.

Sartre, J.-P., 52, 83
Schleiermacher, F. D. E., 90
Schulz, Walter, 94n.
Smith, R. Gregor, 38n., 48
Socrates, 61, 68, 114
Solomon, King, 70
Stephen, J. K., 97n.
Strauss, D. F., 92

Tate and Brady, 105n.
Tavard, G. H., 50n.
Taylor, John V., 48
Temple, William, 20
Thomas, J. Heywood, 50n.
Tillich, Paul, 50-2, 55, 81, 88n., 96
Twain, Mark, 102

Warnock, G. J., 85n.
Warren, M. A. C., 36n., 48
Watt, W. Montgomery, 17n.
Weizsäcker, C. F. von, 45, 48
Williams, N. P., 23
Wingren, Gustaf, 84n.
Wittgenstein, L., 57n.
Wootton, Barbara, 52n.
Wordsworth, W., 97n.

Xenophanes, 13